Winning Grants Step by Step

The Complete Workbook for Planning, Developing, and Writing Successful Proposals

FOURTH EDITION

Tori O'Neal-McElrath

JB JOSSEY-BASS™

A Wiley Brand

Cover design by Michael Cook
Cover image © Ankur Patil/iStockphoto

Published by Jossey-Bass
A Wiley Brand

One Montgomery Street, Suite 1200, San Francisco, CA 94104-4594—www.josseybass.com

Jossey-Bass books and products are available through most bookstores. To contact Jossey-Bass directly call our Customer Care Department within the U.S. at 800-956-7739, outside the U.S. at 317-572-3986, or fax 317-572-4002.

Wiley also publishes its books in a variety of electronic formats and by print-on-demand. Some material included with standard print versions of this book may not be included in e-books or in print-on-demand. If the version of this book that you purchased references media such as CD or DVD that was not included in your purchase, you may download this material at http://booksupport.wiley.com. For more information about Wiley products, visit www.wiley.com.

Library of Congress Cataloging-in-Publication Data

O'Neal-McElrath, Tori, date.
    Winning grants step by step : the complete workbook for planning, developing, and writing successful proposals / Tori O'Neal-McElrath. — Fourth edition.
      pages cm. — (The Jossey-Bass nonprofit guidebook series)
    Includes bibliographical references and index.
    ISBN 978-1-118-37834-2 (paper/website)
    1. Proposal writing for grants. 2. Nonprofit organizations—Finance. I. Carlson, Mim, date. Winning grants. II. Title.
    HG177.C374 2013
    658.15'224—dc23

                                      2013014312

Printed in the United States of America

FOURTH EDITION

PB Printing   10 9 8 7 6 5 4 3

The Jossey-Bass Nonprofit Guidebook Series

The Jossey-Bass Nonprofit Guidebook Series provides new
to experienced nonprofit professionals and volunteers
with the essential tools and practical knowledge they
need to make a difference in the world. From hands-on
workbooks to step-by-step guides on developing a critical skill or learning how to perform an important task or
process, our accomplished expert authors provide readers
with the information required to be effective in achieving
goals, mission, and impact.

Contents

Website Contents

Worksheet 1.1: Proposal Idea Questionnaire
Worksheet 2.1: Letter of Inquiry Questionnaire
Worksheet 3.1: Statement of Problem Questionnaire
Worksheet 4.1A: Goals and Objectives Exercise
Worksheet 5.1: Methods Exercise
Worksheet 6.1: Evaluation Planning Questionnaire
Worksheet 7.1: Future Funding Questionnaire
Worksheet 8.1: Revenue and Expense Budget
Worksheet 9.1: Organization Background Exercise
Worksheet 10.1: Summary Questionnaire
Worksheet 11.1: Final Proposal Checklist
Budget Template: Multiyear
Budget Template: One Year
Budget Template: Swim 4 Life Program
Sample Proposal: Capacity Building for Museum Consultant
Sample Proposal: Common Grant Application for Autism Program
Sample Proposal: Electronic Application for Deaf Teen Pregnancy
    Prevention
Sample Proposal: Electronic Application for Disease Advocacy
    Program
Sample Letter of Intent: To a New Prospect for Scholarships
Sample Letter of Introduction: For a Food Bank's Expansion
Resource A: What Is a Foundation?
Resource B: How to Research Funders
Resource C: Resources for Grantseekers

List of Figures, Samples, and Worksheets

Acknowledgments

THIS WORKBOOK IS a coming together of all aspects of the winning grants process: prospect research, program planning, grantwriting, proposal submission and follow up, and relationship building and stewardship. In this fourth edition, *Winning Grants Step by Step* will continue to augment the many workshops and clinics and the various forms of consultation available on proposal writing.

Special acknowledgments specific to this fourth edition go to three extraordinary individuals, all of whom were also strong devotees of the first three editions of this workbook. Ashyia Johnson is a contributing author to this edition, serving as the primary writer for Step 8 (Budgets). Ashyia brings over fifteen years of finance and budget experience in both public and private sectors. She has spent the past five years in project management and leadership roles in the federal government, where her primary focus is on budgetary and financial matters. She is also an active member of several nonprofit volunteer organizations, including Delta Sigma Theta, Inc., Jack and Jill of America, Inc., and the Junior League of Washington where she serves in various roles that involve financial and program planning, as well as fundraising. Sheryl Kaplan is back again from the third edition to contribute several sample proposals for successfully funded grants. Sheryl is an eighteen-year veteran as a grantwriting consultant and has her own consulting practice, SKaplan Grants. Patricia Sinay is a second contributing author to this edition, and is the primary writer for Step 4 (Goals and Objectives). She brings more than twenty years of experience working with nonprofits and foundations. She now runs Community Investment Strategies, a consulting firm she founded where she specializes in collaboratives, board development, nonprofit capacity building, and philanthropic program development. Patricia teaches a class on public service at the University of California, San Diego, and is in frequent demand as a speaker and facilitator at conferences and workshops.

The Author

TORI O'NEAL-McELRATH has more than twenty-five years of experience in the areas of organizational development, fundraising, program design and implementation, and capacity building with a broad range of nonprofit organizations and foundations. Since 2009, Tori has served as the Director of Institutional Advancement at the Center for Community Change (CCC), a national nonprofit focused on building the power and capacity of low-income people, especially low-income people of color, to have a significant impact in improving their communities and the policies and institutions that affect their lives. Prior to joining the senior management team at CCC, she was the founding principal of O'Neal Consulting, a full-service organizational development practice that specialized in multi-funder collaborations, board development, fundraising, strategic planning, and interim executive leadership. She has successfully raised millions of dollars from foundations, corporations, and individuals throughout her years as a consultant, staff person, board member, and volunteer. Over the years, Tori has taught major gifts fundraising while on the faculty of the University of California Los Angeles Extension, and grantsmanship, annual fund campaigns, and nonprofit management workshops through various volunteer centers. She has served as a presenter and facilitator at numerous local, state, and national conferences, and was most recently a contributing author to *Nonprofit 101: A Complete and Practical Guide for Leaders and Professionals* (a Wiley Publication).

How to Use This Workbook

WINNING GRANTS STEP BY STEP, Fourth Edition will walk the reader, step by step as the title implies, through the basic grantwriting process and will clearly illustrate that conducting thorough research up front, following directions, building relationships, and implementing sound program planning is what best positions organizations to win grants. By employing the strategies as outlined, grantseekers will significantly increase their ability to turn organizational programs, projects, and even general operating needs into proposals worthy of the full consideration of funders.

This is a hands-on, user-friendly workbook that guides the user through the various stages of development that will enable organizations to take an idea or concept and make it come to life in the form of a proposal. Real-life examples, samples of materials, worksheets to support grantseekers as they create materials, and helpful tips can be found throughout the workbook. Guidelines, suggestions, and exercises prepare the reader to tackle proposal development for various organizations in the nonprofit arena—community-based agencies, educational institutions, hospitals and clinics, and research organizations. "Reality Checks" and "Helpful Hints" offer brief focused guidance. "Definitions," unless otherwise stated, are provided by the Nonprofit Good Practice Guide (www.npgoodpractice.org/Glossary), a project of the Johnson Center at Grand Valley State University. One of the new features of *Winning Grants Step by Step, Fourth Edition* is that it has a companion website, josseybass.com/go/winninggrants. This website contains all of the worksheets found at the end of each chapter, live links to the references provided in Resource C (Resources for Grantseekers), and sample proposals.

Ultimately, the worksheets and other activities are crafted to assist in developing proposals and letters of inquiry to meet the requirements of funding institutions of various types—corporate, private, operating, family, and community.

Winning Grants Step by Step, Fourth Edition is crafted with three kinds of individuals in mind: (1) entry-level grantwriters, (2) other organizational staff and volunteers with limited knowledge or experience of grantwriting, and

(3) people with some experience who are seeking a refresher in "grantwriting 101." Though grantwriting basics can be generally applied to all types of grant processes, this workbook focuses primarily on foundation grants, with some limited focus on corporate grants. Several resources on other sorts of grants can be found in the Resources for Grantseekers section on the website.

This workbook is modeled on creating proposals for program funding, and can easily be adapted for general support and other proposals as well. *Winning Grants Step by Step, Fourth Edition* targets this basic truth: a grant proposal must clearly articulate a well thought out, well-crafted program that both inspires confidence in the nonprofit's ability to successfully implement it and fits within the interests of the funders who will receive it. Funders are looking to make strategic investments with their limited grant resources, and they need to see a direct connection between the organization's program and community need(s) being met—and they need to see how grantseekers will track and measure their success.

Almost every organization out there addressing community needs has good ideas. The key to winning grants is to match those good ideas with funders who are interested in the same actions and outcomes.

Step One of this workbook walks grantseekers through the process of developing a proposal idea.

Step Two provides guidance on introducing a project to possible funders, as well as some helpful ideas about ways to develop relationships with funders, which is a critical component in winning grants.

Steps Three through Ten focus on the specific process components that will take ideas from a concept to an effective proposal.

Step Eleven walks grantseekers through the final step in the process, submitting a proposal.

Step Twelve focuses on how to sustain relationships with funders after the grantmaking process has concluded—whether the program was funded or not.

Finally, the Resources for Grantseekers section, which can be found both in the book and on the companion website, addresses key components of the grantseeking process, such as prospect research, and offers a number of direct links to directories, guides, tutorials, portals, and actual foundation websites, as well as other websites deemed potentially helpful to the users of this workbook.

Incorporated throughout *Winning Grants Step by Step, Fourth Edition* are samples that are intended to highlight what a particular step is addressing. These samples focus on the work of the Swim 4 Life program, whose mission is to empower youth in the underserved communities throughout King County, Any State, through high-quality programs to utilize the discipline of swimming to improve physical fitness, nurture self-esteem, and acquire the confidence to advance their lives. The Swim 4 Life program is fictitious, but based on a similar real-life organization.

The best way to use *Winning Grants Step by Step, Fourth Edition* is to actually go through it step by step, crafting a grant proposal along the way. This workbook is unique in that is structured to follow a process typically used when preparing a proposal; grantseekers can develop a proposal of their own while reading the book and completing the exercises.

Remember, there is no magic to navigating the grantseeking process or to preparing successful proposals. These activities simply take good planning, good writing, good research, and an approach that is geared to a prospective funder with whom the organization has developed a good relationship.

Introduction
An Overview of the Grantseeking Process

LET'S START WITH THE OBVIOUS: every nonprofit organization, from start-ups to well-established, local community organizations to national affiliate organizations, consider foundation grants both a desirable and essential source of funding support. Compared to other revenue generating options, grants appear to take less effort and yield a larger reward. In many respects, that is true. However, the word "appear" is important: while grant seeking is relatively inexpensive in comparison to other fundraising strategies and can, in fact, yield large award amounts, it does have expenses associated with it, including a significant amount of dedicated staff (and possibly consulting) time for research, program planning, budgeting, and attention to details and various deadlines. A strong proposal—that is, a well-written, well-organized, and concise proposal—can bring in substantial income for organizational programs.

That being said, not every organization is ready to pursue or receive grant funding. So before an organization starts on the path of seeking grant funding, or attempts to move up from smaller grants to grants of larger amounts, the staff and board should ask itself: Is the organization ready for grant funding or a significant increase in grant funding?

Organizational leadership should start by answering these five sets of questions:

1. Are the organization's mission, purpose, and goals already well-established and articulated? Does the organization have its strategic plan or annual operating plan in place?

2. Does the organization have solid financial procedures and systems in place? Does it have the ability to effectively track, monitor, and report on how it expends both restricted and unrestricted grant funds?

3. Does the organization have the necessary staff in place to ensure that it can deliver on its stated goals and objectives? Can it do what it promises? If not, does the staff leadership possess the ability to effectively get the right staff in place should the organization be awarded a grant?

4. Is the organizational leadership prepared to do what it takes to meet the requirements that come with receiving grant funding? These requirements may vary greatly depending on the amount and source of the funding, and might include some or all of the following: producing quarterly, semiannual, or annual progress reports (including financial updates relative to the grant); conducting ongoing program evaluation; participating in special training; and attending conferences and meetings (particularly if the funding relates to a special initiative of a foundation). Meeting grant expectations might also require the organization to expand its services, increase its office space, and support staff expansion (with human resources efforts, information technology, and training).

5. Does the organization have solid access to—and understanding of—technology? Foundations of all sizes and focus areas are switching to online submission processes, and many conduct nearly all of their communication with their grantees and prospective grantees via email. In addition, does the organization have an online presence in the form of a website? While not a mandatory tool with most foundations, an organization with a website presents as technologically "in step." An organization needs to honestly assess whether it has the basic technology in place to communicate with funders and access and engage in the grantseeking process online.

If an organization can answer yes to these five groups of questions, it is well positioned to begin the grantseeking process.

In many instances a well-prepared and clearly articulated proposal can build an organization's credibility with grantmakers, whether the organization is initially successful in securing a grant or not. Nonprofits that have the respect of grantmakers are often proactively sought after to work on issues of particular concern to both themselves and the funders. Often this funder solicitation comes in the form of a targeted funder initiative. This provides both the grantmaker and the nonprofit with a unique opportunity to collaborate on a larger scale than they would under an individual grant.

More funders of all types (public, private, and operating foundations, as well as some government funders) are engaging in community or issue convenings, or both, as a routine part of their work. Participation in these types of convenings is another solid way to engage potential funders.

Grantseeking is, naturally, the most popular way for nonprofits to secure funding for programs; however, it is but one of several ways an organization can potentially raise funds. There are many different fundraising campaigns that may increase revenues—and visibility—for an organization, including (but not limited to) direct mail and email efforts, social media strategies involving Facebook, Twitter, and various other social media outlets, mobile strategies, membership drives, work place giving, special events, donor giving clubs, "thons" (as in walk-a-thons, dance-a-thons, and jump-a-thons), and more. These strategies should all be kept in mind in addition to grantseeking as a part of a well-rounded fundraising plan. Not only is a diversified fundraising plan something grantmakers like to see, but it is vital to a nonprofit's ongoing work, as gaining support is important to build shared ownership in the nonprofit by constituents and other supporters, so it remains well grounded. Also, grantseeking is a process that takes time. Some grant cycles take as long as six months from the time a grant proposal is submitted to the time an organization learns whether it has been funded. Then, if an organization is awarded a grant, it might take up to another few weeks before funding is received—which is increasingly being done by wire transfer as opposed to mailing a paper check (once again a reference to the increased need for organizations to have appropriate technology in place). If an organization is in need of immediate funds, writing a grant proposal is not the most effective way to raise it in most cases, although there is always an exception to the rule.

Nonprofit organizations have seen some fairly significant shifts in the funding climate over the last few years, but one thing remains the same, particularly for larger organizations: the vast majority of the funds raised in the private sector come from individuals, not foundations. The chart in Figure I.1 illustrates this point.

Government funding, delivered through grants from federal, state, and local agencies, adds billions of public dollars that are not factored into the chart in Figure I.1. That said, government funds are typically offered for projects aimed at very narrow target audiences and qualifications, so grantseekers should do their homework to ensure that there is indeed a match worth investing the time to produce these typically onerous grant proposals—it will most certainly take time and clear intention, not to mention the fairly significant due diligence to steward this kind of funding once secured.

FIGURE I.1

2011 Contributions: $298.42 Billion by Source of Contributions (in billions of dollars—all figures are rounded)

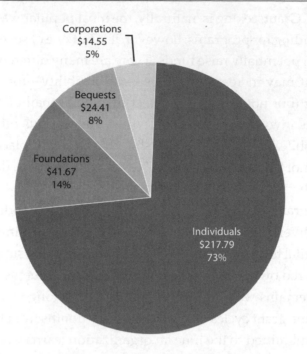

Corporations
$14.55
5%

Bequests
$24.41
8%

Foundations
$41.67
14%

Individuals
$217.79
73%

Source: Giving USA Foundation, Giving USA 2011: The Executive Summary of the Annual Report on Philanthropy for the Year 2011. Glenview, Ill.: Giving USA Foundation, 2012.

Reality Check

All foundations are not created equal. Many—though by no means all—national foundations are, by and large, directing the lion's share of their grants to larger organizations (national nonprofits, including those with affiliates throughout the nation, major universities, hospitals, museums, and the like). Yet there are literally thousands of local, regional, and statewide foundations that fund various-sized organizations. Smaller and mid-sized foundations are often located in the very communities of the organizations themselves. Therefore, organizations seeking grants need to be diligent about conducting thorough prospect research up front and before the first word is written for any new grant proposals. This is also all the more reason for grantseekers to state their case clearly throughout its proposal.

Categories of Support

Organizations are dynamic and have varied financial needs, which typically fall into one of the following categories:

- *Operating* (general support or unrestricted income). This is the funding nonprofits need to pay rent, utilities, and the other everyday costs associated with running the organization—the basics that allow it to fulfill its mission. Typically, the sources of general operating funds are individuals (through annual fund campaigns, direct mail campaigns, and special events), earned income, and grants.

- *Program* (temporarily restricted income). Program or special project funding is of primary interest to most grantmakers, be they foundations, corporations, or even government agencies. It is funding that organizations receive to start a new program, continue running or expanding an existing program, or launch a time-limited project.

- *Capacity building.* This special project funding is used for a targeted effort to increase an organization's capacity to better support its mission and fulfill its particular administrative or fundraising goals. Some foundations are willing to invest in capacity-building grants to organizations doing great work.

- *Capital or equipment.* Funds for capital support are often raised through a targeted fundraising drive known as a capital campaign or through seeking special equipment grants. These intensive efforts—designed to generate a specified amount of funds within a specified time period for construction, remodeling and renovation, building expansion, or the purchase of land or equipment—typically involve large scale individual major gift solicitations, followed by substantial support from foundations and corporations. Some government agencies also provide funds for capital projects.

- *Endowments.* Funds for endowments are often generated through bequests and planned gifts; that is, through giving by an individual to an organization under the terms of a will or trust. Endowment funds may also be received as part of a capital or endowment campaign, using the methods for raising capital or equipment funds. In some cases, a longtime funder dedicated to an organization over a period of time may be willing to make an endowment grant, which may be a way to solidify their support of said nonprofit or may be a part of an exit strategy on the part of the grantmaker, particularly if they have been funding the nonprofit for a while. Generally the endowment principal is held as a long-term investment for the organization, and the interest income is used each year for operating needs.

There are other categories of support that might be considered under one of the categories already outlined or might be stand-alone. These include

- *Planning.* This is the funding nonprofits need to support a continuing process of analyzing program data, making decisions, and formulating plans for action in the future, aimed at achieving program goals.

- *Research.* Funds awarded to institutions to cover costs of investigation and clinical trials. Research grants for individuals are usually referred to as fellowships.

Definitions

Earned income. "Money received by an organization in return for the sale of a product or rendered service."

Capacity building. "The development of an organization's core skills and capabilities, such as leadership, management, finance and fundraising, programs, and evaluation, in order to build the organization's effectiveness and sustainability."

The Proposal Process

There is no secret or trick to writing a winning grant proposal. The keys to success are

- Documenting an unmet community need, which the grantseeker is in a position to address
- Developing a clear plan for the program (or operations growth or capital work)
- Researching funders thoroughly
- Building strong relationships with funders
- Targeting proposals carefully
- Writing a concise proposal

Whether preparing a proposal for a foundation or a corporation, the process of proposal writing will be essentially the same. Organizations will

- Identify an unmet need that said organization can or should address
- Determine if other organizations within the community they service are currently attempting to address this unmet need
- Develop the plan to meet the need
- Determine whether there are potential partners or collaborators
- Identify potential funders and begin to build relationships with them
- Write the proposals, with each being tailored specifically for one potential funder
- Engage in strategic follow-up once the proposal has been submitted

This book covers the proposal process in detail in Steps One through Twelve. The major components of a proposal are as follows:

- *Cover letter:* a short letter that accompanies the proposal and briefly describes its significance

- *Executive summary* (or *proposal summary* or *summary):* a very brief (usually one to two pages) overview of the proposal

- *Problem statement* (or *statement of need* or *need statement):* a compelling description of the need to be addressed by the grantseeker

- *Organization background* (or *background statement):* a presentation of the nonprofit's qualifications to carry out the proposed project

- *Goals and objectives:* a description of what the organization ultimately hopes to accomplish with a program (goal), and a spelling out of the specific results or outcomes to be accomplished (objectives)

- *Methods* (or *strategies):* a description of the programs, services, and activities that will achieve the desired results

- *Evaluation:* a plan for assessing program accomplishments

- *Sustainability:* a presentation of the nonprofit's strategies for developing additional funding to continue the program after the initial grant funding is over

- *Budget:* a line-item summary and narrative of program revenues and expenses

A proposal's format and length will vary depending on the grantmaker. In general, proposals contain the same key components to help funders understand that an organization has a sound plan that meets an important need and will make a positive impact on whomever it serves. The format laid out in this book is commonly used among funders but is by no means the only format possible. In fact, as previously mentioned, many funders large and small are moving to an online grant proposal process. These processes, while sometimes limiting an organization's ability to go deeper in explanation and details due to space limits, typically follow to a large degree the step-by-step process outlined in this book.

The step-by-step process is a useful and hands-on way to develop an organization's thoughts and present its program. After following these well-defined steps, it will be much easier to put the results into whatever order the funder requests. The importance of following each grantmaker's guidelines cannot be emphasized enough. These guidelines will walk grantseekers through each funder's requirements for proposal development, packaging, and submission. The proposals on the *Winning Grants Step by Step, Fourth Edition* website show some of the different formats required by different funders. Many foundations belong to a regional association of grantmakers (RAG); RAGs provide education, networking, and services to their members and advocate for foundations' interests and concerns with policymakers. Members of a RAG may use a common statewide or regional application form (some examples of which can be found on the website), which makes the process of grantseeking easier. Be sure to check with your local RAG to find out if common applications exist in your area.

Types of Proposals

Broadly speaking, there are three types of proposals.

A *letter of intent* (or *letter of inquiry*) is generally a two- or three-page summary (though some funders may request a specific number of pages) submitted when the funder wishes to see a brief description of the project before deciding whether to ask for a longer, more detailed proposal. This document must focus on how the proposed project fits the priorities of the funder. It should also clearly describe the need and outline the plan to meet it.

A letter proposal is the type most often requested by corporations. It is typically a three- or four-page description of the project plan, the organization requesting the funds, and the actual request. The letter proposal and the letter of intent are often confused by grantseekers. The difference between a letter proposal and a letter of intent is this: In the letter proposal grantseekers are actually requesting funds. In the letter of intent grantseekers are only introducing their idea to the funder in order to determine whether the funder has an interest in receiving a more detailed proposal.

The *long proposal* (or *full proposal*), a format that includes a cover letter and a proposal summary, is the type most often requested by foundations. Corporations should not receive this format unless they specifically request it. Long proposals range from five to twenty-five pages, with most funders being interested in receiving about seven to ten pages, plus attachments. In the longer proposal, the grantseeker has an opportunity to give many details about the project and its importance to the community. When using this longer format, grantseekers should make sure that the funding request—the actual dollar amount—is not hidden. It should appear in the cover letter and in the summary as well as in the body of the proposal.

Foundations employing an online grant submission process will abide by much of what is outlined above, although the space for each step is likely to be more condensed than a typical document proposal, so grantseekers should be prepared for that eventuality.

Tips for Writing Proposals

There are three basic things grantseekers should keep in mind when conceiving their proposals:

1. Picture the reader of the grant as a friendly and fairly educated person who hasn't been around in a while and doesn't have a clue about the work of the organization, but she's interested. What would the grantseeker share to transfer excitement and a sense of mission?

2. Be sure to use compelling facts, but equally important, be sure to tell compelling stories that highlight what the organization does, how it does what it does, and why it matters. Put a face, place, and situation to the facts to make them real.

3. Always keep in mind that a grant is not just a grant; it is an investment on the part of the funder. Foundations have limited resources and are focused on advancing the foundation's mission. Therefore, it is important to their board and the larger community that they make smart investments.

The heart and soul of an organization's proposal will come from those who have identified the problem or unmet need and conceptualized the program to address it; they must be an integral part of the proposal development process. Grantseekers need to decide on one person to write the proposal—either the staff person with the strongest writing skills or an outside grantwriter—and have that person working closely with those who developed the program to be funded. Keep in mind that the proposal will suffer if the writer selected—whether internal staff or outside grantwriter—does not have an understanding of what the project is, why it is important to the community, and why the organization seeking funding is best qualified to undertake the project. And even when the writer does have this understanding, it is essential to have the program staff involved in the development of the grant proposal.

Stick to the following principles when preparing the proposal:

- *Follow the grant guidelines.* Organizations do not want their proposal dismissed on a technicality, which happens more than most grantseekers think. It is common for grantmakers to make explicit the format they want followed. Make the proposal visually attractive, but do not overdo it. Whenever possible, break up the written page. Use a reasonable font size, and use bulleted lists and other formatting tools to make each page look inviting—but follow the instructions outlined by each individual funder.

- *Get the facts straight.* Make sure data are relevant and up-to-date to support the need for the program. General data to help set a framework for the statement of need are worthwhile, but the most important data are the facts and figures specific to the geographical area served, target audience, and other key elements.

- *Do not make the organization's proposal so bleak that the reader sees no point in trying to address the problem.* Use an affirming writing style, and present a well-reasoned, thoughtful presentation. A grant proposal should contain some elements of emotional appeal yet also be realistic and factual.

- *Be aware that many grantmakers read the executive summary first, followed closely by the program budget.* If they go beyond the executive summary and budget—congratulations; at a minimum their interest is sparked. For this reason, grantseekers should consider developing the proposal summary last.

- *KISS (Keep It Sweet and Simple).* Avoid jargon and do not overwrite. Make it easy for someone who probably is not an expert in a particular field to read, understand, and successfully digest the entire proposal. Jargon (specialized words that only people in the relevant field will understand) acts as a barrier to understanding, and people cannot be sympathetic to things they cannot comprehend. Be thrifty with words, particularly now in the age of online proposals, where word limits are typically in place, but do not sacrifice information that is critical to making the case for the project.

- *Get some honest feedback on the proposal before submitting it to a funder.* Ask one or two people (maybe a staff or board member or even someone outside your organization) to review the proposal carefully. Does everything make sense? Is the need clear? Do the proposed objectives (Step Four) and methods (Step Five) seem to be an appropriate response to the identified unmet need? Use the answers to these questions to strengthen the final proposal.

- *Remember that one size does **not** fit all.* After developing a proposal, study the guidelines of each prospective funder identified as a possible match for the program and tailor the proposal for each one accordingly. It is true that most funders want the same basic information. That said, it is also true that they request it in different formats, which will require reordering sections, cutting and pasting, and possibly relabeling some sections (for instance, the problem statement may become the need statement). Occasionally, additional material may need to be added or some material deleted from the original version. By tailoring the proposal for each funder, each proposal reviewer will potentially be provided with confidence that the proposal is responding to the specific grantmaker's concerns.

- *Plan ahead.* The grantseeking process typically operates within six-month to nine-month windows, and each funder operates on its own schedule. From the time a proposal is submitted to the time a potential funder responds will be on average six months, and many funders have specific deadlines for receiving proposals. Develop a calendar that lists all foundation and corporation prospects and their deadlines. Also maintain a list of each funder's priorities that seem applicable to the organization's desired program, and then be sure to clearly spell out the parts of the organization's program that fit those priorities. This calendar will help grantseekers stay organized and on track as numerous deadline dates and priority areas are juggled.

Step 1
Developing the Proposal Idea

NOW THAT AN INTRODUCTION to the process of preparing a proposal has been given, let's take that first step! This section of the workbook walks grantseekers through developing the proposal idea by answering some key questions. Before beginning to write a proposal to secure funds to address an unmet need, grantseekers must first determine which programs in the organization are the most "fundable." That is, which programs are most likely to garner the most interest from grantmakers?

Many funders have a fairly strong preference for investing in new programs and successful continuing programs that are expanding over general operating support or basic program continuation. Again, be sure to do a thorough job of researching prospective funders so that there is a sense of clarity specific to the audience with which the organization has to work. Funders might also have an interest in a special project, such as a new time-specific project, a capacity-building idea, a set of technology improvements, or technical assistance. This workbook uses the idea of expanding a successful pilot program as the model for developing a proposal.

To start developing a proposal idea, begin with the end in mind. The organization has identified an unmet need, or wants to expand on a program already in existence that is successfully meeting an unmet need. So sit down with everyone involved to begin to flesh out this program idea— how an organization is going to meet, or grow the existing program to continue meeting, that unmet need it has identified. Use a team approach in developing the plan and involve the appropriate staff, clients, and volunteers *from the very beginning.* The team can develop an initial program plan first or expansion plan, which then will become the basis of the entire proposal.

The importance of having the right people at the table when the program plan is developed cannot be emphasized enough. One of the worst things

Helpful Hint

General operating support. While still not as available as is needed in the nonprofit arena, there is a growing movement on the part of some funders to invest in general operating support. Be diligent in the research phase of grantseeking to uncover those funders receptive to receiving a general operating proposal.

that can happen to a nonprofit is to be funded for a program that it then discovers it does not have the ability to successfully implement or, worse yet, a program that does not effectively meet the needs initially identified because it was developed in a vacuum—or in the development director's office—rather than with the individuals who will be responsible for implementing it.

When preparing a proposal, many writers start with the planning sections (problem statement, goals and objectives, methods, evaluation, program sustainability, and budget) because these sections form the core of the proposal. Then they write the organization background section, finishing with the summary and the cover letter. This workbook follows that format, which is easily adaptable to online proposal submissions as well.

The planning sections of the proposal deserve careful attention; without a clearly articulated program plan, it is nearly impossible to get funding. Writing a clear, goal-oriented, thoughtful proposal is crucial. If a grantseeker can't clearly and effectively explain what they're doing, why they're doing it, and how they're going to do it in a way that is easily understandable, staff at grantmaking institutions will not have what they need to advocate on the organization's behalf.

A guideline here is that nonprofits should expect to focus approximately 70 percent of their time on program planning; the other 30 percent can be dedicated to writing and packaging the proposal. Also, the tighter an organization's program plan, the easier the proposal will be to write. Go into this process knowing that even with all of the planning, fine-tuning of the plan will be necessary as the proposal is being developed—this is common practice.

Logic Models in Program Design

What exactly is a logic model? A logic model is a valuable tool that produces a basic program picture that shows how the organization's program is intended to work. The tool also helps organizations outline the sequence of related events in their programs. These events provide a direct and visual connection between the need for the planned program and the desired results and outcomes expected from the program. A logic model can be particularly useful when it comes to designing the evaluation for a new program. More information on logic models, including examples and online tools, can be found on the website, including actual logic model building portals.

Reality Check

Check the fit. When conducting prospect research, grantseekers are bound to come across many wonderful opportunities presented by grantmakers—special initiatives and pots of funding for specific programs and projects within defined fields of interest. And even though they might sound exciting and worthwhile, always measure every funding opportunity by the organization's mission. Is there really a fit—a natural fit? Or is the organization "growing another foot" to fit the "shoe" the funder has to offer? Always, always use the organization's mission and organizational purpose as the primary guide.

To get started on developing a compelling proposal idea, complete Worksheet 1.1. The more thorough the answers, the more helpful the worksheet will be. After answering the questions in Worksheet 1.1, use those answers to identify one specific idea to develop using the exercises in this book. To check the merit of the idea identified, ask the Proposal Development Review Questions at the end of this step. Then follow Steps Two through Twelve to create a well-planned proposal. Throughout these steps, this workbook will refer grantseekers to the accompanying website for worksheet examples and templates.

WORKSHEET 1.1:
Proposal Idea Questionnaire

1. What new projects is your organization planning for the next two to three years?

    Project A:

    Project B:

    Project C:

    Project D:

2. Which of these projects are most compatible with your organization's current mission and purpose, and in what way?

    Project   Compatibility

    A

    B

    C

    D

3. What is unique about your organization's project?

    Project   Uniqueness

    A

    B

    C

    D

WORSHEET 1.1:
Proposal Idea Questionnaire (Continued)

4. What other organizations are doing this project? Is there duplication of effort? Is there potential for collaboration?

Duplicate Project   Possible Collaboration Project
(with whom)   (with whom)

A

B

C

D

5. What community need does each of your organization's projects address?

Project   Need Addressed

A

B

C

D

6. What members of your community—including civic leaders, political figures, the media, your organization's clients or constituents, and other nonprofits—support each project?

Project   Supporters

A

B

C

D

WORKSHEET 1.1:
Proposal Idea Questionnaire (Continued)

7. Does your organization currently have the expertise to undertake each project? If new staff is necessary, can the organization manage growth in infrastructure (HR, technology, supervisory oversight, and so forth) effectively? (Check each category that applies to each project.)

Project	Expertise	HR	Technology	Other (specify)
A				
B				
C				
D				

8. Is there internal (board and staff) support for the project? External support (community leaders, clients, neighbors, and so forth)? (Check the category that applies to each project and specify the type of support.)

Project	Internal Support (specify)	External Support (specify)
A		
B		
C		
D		

Proposal Development Review Questions

To find out whether the proposal idea being presented has merit, answer the following six questions:

1. What community need does the program or service that the organization has identified address? (The answer to this question will become the framework for the proposal's need statement.)

2. What would an improved community situation look like? (This answer will become the basis of the proposal's goals and objectives.)

3. What can the organization do to improve this situation? (This answer will become the basis of the proposal's methods.)

4. How will the organization know if its program or service has succeeded? (This answer will become the basis of the proposal's program evaluation.)

5. How much will the organization's program or service cost, and what other sources of funding will it have? (This answer will become the basis of the proposal's program budget.)

6. How will the organization's program or service be funded in the future? (This answer will become the basis of the proposal's program sustainability.)

Now that the organization's proposal idea is successfully identified and framed, let's move on to Step Two, which addresses a critical part of winning grants: developing relationships with funders.

Step 2
Developing Relationships with Funders

BUILDING RELATIONSHIPS WITH FUNDERS is a long-term, sincere, and strategic investment of time and intention. Once it is determined that an organization's proposed program is solid, time and focused effort needs to be invested in identifying funders who are potentially a match with both the organization and its proposed program, project, or special initiative. Resources on the *Winning Grants Step by Step, Fourth Edition* website offer links to other sites with detailed information and tips on how to effectively conduct prospect research to successfully identify possible funders. Step Two also provides no-nonsense advice about prospect research and then offers ideas for developing relationships once funders are identified. Please refer to Resource A (What Is a Foundation?) to learn more about what foundations are and how they work.

Making the Initial Approach

A grantmaker's website typically holds all the information grantseekers need to determine whether it is a match. In fact, in this day and age, it is now fairly commonplace for all grant guidelines and supporting materials to be on the website; funders are "going green" in every way and reducing paper consumption. So not only are grant guidelines online but, as mentioned in the Introduction, grant proposals are now routinely submitted online and paperless. Typically, grantseekers will find an abundance of information, including—but by no means limited to—background information on the foundation as an institution, its staff and board of directors, grant guidelines, and special funding initiatives, if any. Most funder websites will also proudly feature current and previous grantees or the programs successfully funded. Foundations, like all 501(c)3 organizations, are required by law to provide access to their Internal Revenue Service Form 990, which is their annual tax return. Many may have a link to this document on their websites, or they can be located by visiting Guide Star (www.guidestar.org) or the Foundation Center (www.foundationcenter.org).

These success stories provide the very best indicators of what specific funders are likely to fund in the future. Some funders may have additional microsites (separate sites that are linked to the main site) for particular funding initiatives they have launched. That said, other funders may still require additional sleuthing on the part of the grantseeker before they can appropriately glean whether there is truly a match. So in addition to reviewing funder websites, grantseekers should use various search engines to research their previous giving to other organizations and perhaps also to look for feature stories about them (if not found on their websites) or pick up the telephone and call a foundation directly.

But be prepared: this conversation just might lead to a brief discussion of the proposed project or program, so the caller should be ready to talk about it and hit the highlights. Who knows? This may be the start of a great new relationship. After reviewing a grantmaker's website and other related materials, determine clarity around there being a potentially solid fit between the organization's proposed program or project and what the grantmaker says it is interested in funding. Grantseekers need to recognize that the relationship they make with foundation staff is one based on mutual need; they then need to be on a mission to educate foundation staff on what they need from the grantseeker's organization.

In addition, it is important not to assume that funders know and understand the grantseeking organization's mission or target audience or that the program being presented is addressing a priority of theirs.

Developing the Relationship

After establishing that there is a good fit, relationship building becomes a continuous process that begins before a single word of a proposal is written, and it spans many years. Keep in mind that it is a relationship, rather than a transaction. Good communication with funders should never end, even if and when the organization may stop receiving grants from them. Once a relationship exists, funders like to receive progress reports about how the organization or program they funded is doing. They may also take an interest in other compelling ideas that the organization has developed.

It's not always easy to develop relationships with funders, especially if they have not previously funded an organization. However, the key is the relationship part of that phrase. It's relationship building, rather than selling, that makes a difference.

Here are a few concrete ways to approach a funder to open the door to relationship building. These are discussed more fully in the following subsections.

- Send the funder a brief email inquiry.
- Call the foundation and speak with someone regarding your proposal idea.
- Send a brief (no longer than two pages maximum) letter of inquiry to the funder.
- Invite the funder to your organization for a site visit.

While grant guidelines determine a nonprofit's initial approach, grantseekers may have a connection to the funder, either directly or through one or more contacts who can potentially open a door on behalf of the organization for an initial meeting or phone conversation.

Reality Check

Be strategic and err on the side of restraint when using a contact to open a door with a funder. Few things are worse than dealing with a program officer who feels pushed into a meeting. Grantseekers always want an invitation, rather than a meeting based on obligation. Think "soft touch" rather than "heavy hand."

Sending Email Inquiries to Funders

Many funders offer grantseekers the option of contacting them via email with questions and funding inquiries. Some grantmakers even provide direct email access to their program officers from their websites; others may have an "info@" email that is routed to the appropriate staff person after review. In either case, email is a valuable tool for stimulating further, more meaningful, contact because it provides an opportunity for a brief introduction as a staff person, as well as the organization represented and the program needing funding. At the same time it gives the program officer the time he needs to review the information and potentially respond. Email is far less demanding for program officers than a phone call and less wasteful than paper documents. And given the significant shift from paper to electronic processes, email is all the more important. The key is to keep it brief! Resist the urge to write a mini proposal in the email. Grantseekers can also request an in-person meeting or time for a phone conversation in the email, which then provides the funder with options for responding to the communication.

Contacting a Funder by Telephone

Before calling a funder to pitch an idea, be prepared. The person with whom a grantseeker speaks may have only a short time for a conversation, so preparation is essential. Be ready to provide the highlights of the organization's program within a ten- to fifteen-minute conversation. This time frame includes the time it may take for the person to ask for clarification of any points. Grantseekers should remember that they are not selling their organization's program to a funder; they are attempting to make a connection between the program and the funding institution's interest areas. To actively build a long-term relationship with the funder and with this particular representative, careful and engaged listening to the funder's needs and providing information the funder wants is extremely important.

In listening to the funder's needs, one might discover—sometimes very early in the conversation—that there in fact is not a match between the organization's program and the funder's current funding priorities; that is why grantseekers should have one or two other program ideas in mind to present as a backup. Do not waste this opportunity with the funder; be fully prepared with information on clearly identified unmet needs that may fit into the funder's interest areas.

Writing a Letter of Inquiry

A letter of inquiry (or LOI) is sometimes the first step in a funder's grant-making process, particularly if the relationship between prospective grantee and funder is new. An LOI provides the funder with a "sneak peek" at the organization, target audience, and prospective program, without requiring the grantseeker to develop a full proposal at this early stage. After the funder has reviewed the information presented in the LOI, the organization may or may not be invited to submit a full proposal. Even though an LOI is a preliminary step, it should be treated as a vital part of relationship building. It is an integral first interaction of what grantseekers hope will be many interactions with the funder. If asked to submit an LOI, check to see whether the funder has specific LOI guidelines. If it does not, the following list suggests what information to include, as a general rule:

- Organization's mission and related programs

- The need the organization wishes to meet

- The outcomes expected from the organization's project

- General details of how an organization will conduct the project

- The potential fit between the funder and the organization

The sample LOI included in this step presents to a funder the Swim 4 Life Program, which will be used as an example program throughout this workbook. This is the letter that the Swim 4 Life program executive director would submit if an LOI was invited by the funder or if the funder accepted unsolicited submissions.

Sample Letter of Inquiry

July 17, 2012
Wendy Wonder
President
XYZ Foundation
0000 Clinton Avenue, Suite 2330
Anytown, Any State 02009

Dear Ms. Wonder:

I appreciate the time Anne Jonas has taken to communicate with us about how our programs fit with the XYZ Foundation's funding priorities, and the encouragement she offered us. Therefore, on behalf of the Board of Directors and staff, I am honored to submit this brief Letter of Inquiry introducing Swim 4 Life, an innovative swimming instruction program by Jane Swimmer, a former U.S. Olympic swimming hopeful and hometown hero. We respectfully request your consideration of a grant of $25,000 to help us expand our programs for low-income youth from two to three schools in the Gathenton School District.

Established as a 501(c)3 organization in 2008, the mission of the Swim 4 Life program is to empower youth in the underserved communities throughout King County through high-quality programs to utilize the discipline of swimming to improve physical fitness, nurture self-esteem, and acquire the confidence to advance their lives. This mission is currently being fulfilled through programs currently operated at Arthur Schomburg Middle School in South Spring and the Rockmore Education Complex High School in Abbington. More than 450 youth have participated since operations began, and we would now like to add Cooperville Middle School, also located in Abbington.

The need for programs like Swim 4 Life is enormous in the communities we serve. Swimming has not been a popular sport in African American or Latino communities in some measure as a result of various factors including access to pools and other safe places to swim. Historically speaking, African Americans were denied access to public pools prior to the civil rights movement—and after in many instances. As a result, this population turned to water holes, ponds, and other unsupervised alternatives, which led to rates of drowning among people of color that far exceed those of whites. For example, according to the Centers for Disease Control and Prevention's latest report in early 2012, the drowning rate for African Americans between the ages of five and fourteen was more than three times that for whites.

Through a range of summer and after-school services, the Swim 4 Life program teaches children to be "water safe" and to swim, and prepares them for competitive team training if they want to further develop their skills. Our program at one school even provides swim instruction specifically for students with disabilities. Our partnership with the Gathenton School District offers us the opportunity to replicate the programs throughout the cities of Rockmore and South Spring in King County, contributing to improved health and fitness of hundreds of youth who have been excluded from the sport because of limited access to safe pools.

With your help, we will expand our program from two to three schools in the Gathenton School District and achieve the following specific programmatic outcomes with the low-income students and students of color we plan to serve in 2012:

- 100 students participate in water aerobics classes, which will enable nonswimmers to participate, since classes are conducted in shallow water

- 25 students are trained as Junior Lifeguards and Lifeguards, including seven at Rockmore Education Complex (a high school)

- 58 students participate on a swim team

- 37 students participate in swim fitness classes, workouts for students who already know how to swim and are looking for an exercise alternative as a part of a healthier lifestyle

- 13 students participate on a water polo team (Note: In previous years, we found that not one of our students even knew what water polo was until the program introduced it as an option)

- 29 students with Individualized Education Programs (IEP) complete the Adapted Learn-to-Swim class

- 39 students complete the Learn-to-Swim class

The outcomes listed above represent a 25% increase in the numbers of students we will serve.

Because of your commitment to encouraging low-income youth and young people of color to reach their fullest potential, as well as your geographic focus in King County, we sincerely hope that the XYZ Foundation will join us as our partner in this important program.

The Swim 4 Life Program budget is $468,800, of which $150,000 remains to be raised. So as you can see, your gift of $25,000 for the expanded program will go a long way toward helping us meet our budget. In addition, investing in Swim 4 Life will make a significant impact on the ability of economically disadvantaged King County, Any State, youth to create a brighter future for themselves. If you have any questions, please feel free to call me at (111) 111–1111. We deeply appreciate your invitation of this Letter of Inquiry and trust that you will see enough of a connection between our program and your foundation's mission that you will invite a full proposal.

Sincerely,
Shawn Jones, Executive Director

Now that a sample LOI has been presented and reviewed, take the time to answer the questions in Worksheet 2.1, which is located both at the end of this chapter and on the *Winning Grants Step by Step, Fourth Edition* companion website, as clearly as possible. This exercise will help in developing a strong letter of inquiry for funders. If grantseekers cannot clearly and articulately answer the questions, that probably means that they need to gather more information before they can effectively complete an LOI.

WORKSHEET 2.1:
Letter of Inquiry Questionnaire

1. What is the purpose of this letter of inquiry? To whom is it being sent, and what is the connection?

2. What year was the organization founded? What year was it incorporated?

3. What is the mission of the organization?

4. What are the long-term goals for the organization?

5. What programs does the organization provide that support these goals?

6. What is the need in the community that you seek funding to address?

7. How, in the organization's view, is the need related to its programs, long-term goals, and mission?

8. What does the organization propose to do about this need?

9. What outcome does the organization anticipate after the first year of funding?

10. What is the total cost of the proposed idea for the first year, or what is the cost to expand the current program? (Or multiple years if you plan to request multiple-year funding?) How much do you want from this funder?

11. Who will be contacting the funder to determine its interest and when? Whom should the funder contact for more information?

Meeting with a Funder

Many grantseekers dream of having face-to-face meetings with prospective funders prior to submitting a proposal because they want not only to get clarification from the funders on key issues but also an opportunity to "prime the pump" and get the grantmakers excited about the program even before they receive the proposal. Unfortunately, preproposal funder meetings are few and far between, because funders simply cannot accommodate every nonprofit's request for them. Also, some funders are leery of these meetings because they do not want to raise unrealistic funding expectations in grantseekers. Managing grantseeker expectations is of the utmost importance to the majority of funders: they certainly want to encourage the submission of solid proposals for programs meeting their interest areas, but they do not want to raise false hope at the same time. Remember: every foundation and corporate grantmaker has a limited amount of funding available for grants every year. That said, if an organization has a contact that already has a strong relationship with a funder, this individual may be able to help broker a meeting. After doing the due diligence of funder research, grantseekers should think about others they know who may also know the funder. Understand also that any early meeting secured with the grantmaker will be very preliminary and in no way ensures that the grantseeker will receive funds from this source.

If an in-person meeting is scheduled, grantseekers should take materials that best describe the organization and the proposed program. In the meeting the grantseeker should attempt to cover the following topics:

- Credibility of the organization
- Need for the proposed project
- Program description
- Community interest in the program
- Proposed outcomes
- Ability to measure success
- Costs and projected revenue sources
- Why this funder's interests may be met by investing in the program

Time with a program officer is likely to be short, so organizations should be prepared to hit the highlights. Listen carefully to the funder's questions and any concerns expressed, and make sure questions are answered fully and truthfully. These questions and concerns should also be addressed again in the proposal that will be submitted following the meeting, provided there is a good fit.

Here are some additional steps to take to develop good relationships with funders with whom the grantseeker has spoken:

- Add the program officer to the organization's mailing list or list serve

- Add the program officer to the organization's newsletter distribution list, and go the extra distance by including a personal note with his newsletter

- Send brief (one- to two-page) progress reports on the successes of the organization's work—ones that the program officer has not funded but that his colleagues at other funding institutions may have funded

- Invite the program officer to organization events with personal notes—even if she cannot come, she will remember the contact

- Contact the program officer occasionally by telephone or email with brief messages and updates. Include quotes or even notes specifically from program constituents

---

Reality Check

Electronic applications. These come in the form of either an actual web-based portal that grantseekers essentially fill out/fill in, and grant guidelines that instruct grantseekers to email the proposal and required attachments, rather than mailing paper copies. The web-based grant proposal portals have a specific space for each proposal component, and they are sometimes limited in the number of words per section. Among funders using electronic applications are the W. K. Kellogg Foundation (www.wkkf.org), The Skoll Foundation (www.skollfoundation.org), The Agnes and Eugene Meyer Foundation (www .meyerfoundation.org/apply-for-funding), and the Hertz Foundation (www.dot hertzfoundation/org/dz /fellowships/application.aspx). Please visit any one of these foundation websites to see clear examples of online application processes. There are more examples located on the *Winning Grants Step by Step, Fourth Edition* website.

Letter of Inquiry Review Questions

1. Is the name of the program and amount of request clearly stated in the first paragraph?

2. Does the second paragraph elaborate further on the proposed project, as well as any related projects (when applicable)?

3. Is the organization's mission statement included?

4. Is the need the proposed program intends to meet clear? Are some preliminary data to support the need for the proposed program included?

5. Are the specific program outcomes the program is targeted to achieve described clearly?

6. Is program implementation included?

7. Is the "fit" or natural connection between the organization's program and the funder's priority areas, as identified in their guidelines, included?

8. If there is some funding already committed to the project, and is it mentioned?

9. Is the program's contact person clearly identified, including all contact information?

Developing relationships with funders is such an important step in the process of winning grants that the value of doing it well cannot be emphasized enough. Now that funder relationships have been explained and helpful hints provided, it's time to develop the problem statement, which is Step Three.

Step 3
Writing a Compelling Problem Statement

THIS STEP HIGHLIGHTS THE KEY ELEMENTS of a *problem statement* (for grantseeking purposes this statement might also be referred to as the *statement of the need* or *need statement*), including the four requirements for it to be successful. The section also offers a worksheet and sample to serve as guides to preparing a problem statement for a proposal.

Purpose of the Problem Statement

What is the problem to be addressed? An organization's problem statement will—or at least it should—directly address this question. Therefore this is the best place to begin writing a proposal. A problem statement sets the framework for the entire proposal, as it describes a critical condition, set of conditions, or a social need affecting certain people or things in a specific place at a specific time. The need statement is fundamental to a proposal because funders must agree with the organization that the program addresses an important community problem. Bolstered by accurate data (quantitative statistics) combined with the right selection of stories that provide a more personal illustration of the need (qualitative data), a compelling need statement is often the first component that motivates a funder to give serious consideration to a nonprofit's request. Make no mistake: a good, solid, and well-supported problem statement is the key that unlocks the door, moving a proposal that much closer to funding consideration.

Finally, the unmet need—and an organization's ability to successfully address it—gives grantmakers an opportunity to realize their own goals.

Content of the Problem Statement

Here are some basic rules to follow when developing the project's problem statement:

- The need being addressed in the statement should have a clear relationship to an organization's mission and purpose.

- The problem statement should focus squarely on those the organization serves and their specific needs, rather than the organization's needs—unless an organizational capacity-building grant is being sought.

- Any assertions about the problem should be well supported with evidence (statistical facts, expert views, trends found in the experience of doing the work, and so on).

- The organization must be able to directly connect—and substantiate—the need described in the proposal with the organization's ability to successfully respond to that need (that ability will be described in a subsequent section of the proposal).

- The problem statement must be easily digestible. Avoid using jargon, and do not make the reader have to work to understand the point. Graphs and charts with data to support the case are often good additions to a proposal, as they present the data in the most compelling way.

The problem being addressed by the organization may be specific to its geographical area or it may be found in many communities. Do not overpromise: if the problem occurs in an area larger than that served by the organization or the proposed program, it is important to focus only on what the organization or program can reasonably accomplish. Should this be the case—the problem exceeds the boundaries of the organization or proposed program—consider positioning the program as a potential model for other nonprofits in other locations. By taking the model approach, an organization broadens the pool of potential funders to include those concerned with the problem in other geographical areas. Consideration should also be given to conducting research to discover whether other organizations in the service area have—or are developing—similar programs to address the same problem. Should this be the case, consider exploring a collaborative program that would leverage and expand the reach of program plans and grant funds.

If the organization decides to take either the model or collaborative approach, highlight this fact in the problem statement; the organization is addressing the need on a larger level through the development of a program that can be a model for others or that it is leveraging its efforts with another organization so it can expand the reach and impact of its program.

Often arts organizations struggle with this section owing to a perception that the arts do not meet a compelling community need. However, arts organizations should be encouraged, as they do meet important needs. Without these nonprofits, certain cultures and traditions would be lost, lives would not be enriched, and young people would not learn new and different ways of expressing themselves. The same holds true for social justice organizations who may struggle with how to quantify social change. Over the last few years, there has been more research in this area, and the website offers some data, studies, and overall guidance on how best to frame social justice outcomes.

For general support grants, there might be a struggle with the problem statement because the proposal addresses the general work of the organization. Focus on describing the problems that the organization addresses: mission and purpose. This, again, goes back to something touched on earlier in this workbook: when focusing on soliciting general operating support, always use the nonprofit's mission and purpose as the guide.

Definition

Collaboration. "A mutually beneficial and well-defined relationship entered into by two or more organizations to achieve common goals. The relationship includes a commitment to mutual relationships and goals, a jointly developed structure and shared responsibility, mutual authority and accountability for success, and sharing of resources and rewards."

Tips for Writing the Problem Statement

The problem statement should be contained to no more than three pages. Being concise with the problem statement will serve grantseekers well, and the reality is that most foundation guidelines limit proposals to ten to twelve pages in total; corporate guidelines typically limit proposals to even fewer pages. Space constricts even more with the online proposal portals, as they literally limit the space to a specific number of words.

In stating the problem, use hard statistics from reputable sources and steer clear of assumptions and undocumented assertions masquerading as legitimate facts.

- *Use statistics that are clear and that document the current unmet need or problem.* If talking about a specific community within a city, offer one or two data points about the city, then zero in on the data specific to that community.

- *Use comparative statistics and research where possible.* Look at the examples in the accompanying Reality Check box. As shown, using data from a community that did something very similar to what the grant-seeker wants to do and citing the benefits that the community derived from the project can make a strong case for the nonprofit to do the same.

- *Quote authorities who have spoken on the topic.* Be sure to cite the person who made each statement and the source where it was found, and if appropriate, provide backup information that substantiates that this person is indeed an authority on the subject matter.

- *Make sure all data collection is well documented.* Grantseekers will use the Internet for research, which is of course more than appropriate. Just make sure that the websites being referenced are reputable and the links are both accurate and current; then clearly cite the sources.

- *Use touching stories of people as examples.* This is very effective, but only when balanced against hard data. Keep in mind that foundations vary in what they seek in terms of the right mix of vignettes and numbers.

- *Give a clear sense of the urgency of the request.* Funders need to understand why the funding is important now.

Take a look at the following Sample Problem Statement from the Swim 4 Life program. Then, using the proposal idea identified and developed in Step One, answer the questions on Worksheet 3.1, as this will assist in beginning to define the need the organization is addressing. After reviewing the Sample Problem Statement and completing the worksheet questionnaire, write the organization's problem statement based on the information developed. Next answer the Problem Statement Review Questions listed at the end of this step to make sure the statement is written well. Rewrite the problem statement until all the review questions are satisfactorily addressed.

Sample Problem Statement

The need for programs like Swim 4 Life is enormous in the communities we serve. Swimming has not been a popular sport in African American or Latino communities in some measure as a result of various factors including access to safe pools. Historically speaking, African Americans were denied access to public pools. As a result, they turned to water holes, ponds, and other unsupervised alternatives, which led to rates of drowning among people of color that far exceed those of whites. For example, according to the Centers for Disease Control and Prevention's latest report in early 2012, the drowning rate for African Americans between the ages of five and fourteen was more than three times that for whites.

To this day, a deep-seated fear about swimming has discouraged African Americans and, to a lesser yet still significant degree, Latinos in the United States from participating in the activity. A story relayed to us by a previous program participant:

> Our family is originally from Louisiana, though many of us moved to Any State after Hurricane Katrina. Those of my family who stayed in Louisiana were having a family picnic a few years ago by a waterway, and not one person at the picnic could swim. A few of the kids were playing at the water's edge when the land gave way and all fell into the water. Nine of my family members died that day—seven kids and two adults who tried to help them. I promised myself that if I ever got the chance, not only would I learn to swim, but I would become a lifeguard.

According to our most recent survey of current and previous program participants, nearly 75 percent of those surveyed have family members who have drowned or experienced a traumatic water incident and are terrified of drowning themselves.

Arthur Schomburg Middle School, one of the program sites, is located in a part of South Spring that offers children and youth little in the way of public resources and facilities for sports, especially swimming. A county facility, Thurgood Marshall Park, 1.7 miles from the school, has a seasonal swim program, open only during the summer even though the pool is indoor and heated. Rosa Parks and Garfield Recreation Centers, twelve miles from the school, have indoor heated pools that open during the summer but are not accessible to young students after school; they would have to cross major thoroughfares to get there.

Most experts agree that children approaching adolescence are particularly vulnerable to peer influences, and for youth living in disadvantaged neighborhoods, the lack of positive opportunities often puts them at risk for gang affiliation, substance abuse, and/or low academic performance. A report issued by the Urban Institute in 2011 detailed the risks, obstacles, and positive strategies needed relative to middle school children from low-income families. According to the study, it is a prime time to introduce innovative and challenging youth sports programs—those not typically available in communities of color—as exciting alternatives to unhealthy risk-taking activities. The Swim 4 Life program in King County, Any State, is designed to take advantage of this age group's interest in experimentation and exploration.

The city of Abbington is served by the program site at the Rockmore Education Complex. It is the most densely populated city in the state, with 8,552 people occupying every square mile, compared with an overall average of 2,093 people per square mile in other cities. It has the highest crime rate in the state, and the poverty rate is 46 percent, nearly twice that of South Spring. Fifty-one percent of children under the age of 18 live in poverty, compared with 31 percent in South Spring, and less than 20 percent the rest of the state. Young people in this city—and South Spring—clearly live under stressful conditions and could benefit greatly from structured and supervised physical activity, as well as safe opportunities for fun and positive engagement. And for all of the reasons outlined, we have selected Cooperville Middle School, also located in Abbington, to expand our program.

A swim program offers many advantages over other physical activities. Swimming is an excellent form of exercise because all the muscles of the body are used, and it requires a constant supply of oxygen to the muscles, making it a mainly aerobic exercise. It is also a gateway to all aquatic sports and is considered one of the important life-saving skills. Many studies such as the one conducted in 2012 by the Center for Research on Effective School for Disadvantaged Youth at the Johns Hopkins University have drawn a connection between participation in structured athletic programs and academic achievement. Yet today, students in local high schools, particularly in the eleventh and twelfth grades, have so many academic requirements that there is not enough time for physical education, even as an elective.

WORKSHEET 3.1:
Statement of Problem Questionnaire

On the Web

Who? Where? When?	What? Why?	Evidence of Problem	Impact If Problems Resolved?
Who is in need (people, animals, land, and so forth)?	Why does this problem exist?	What evidence do you have to support your claim?	What will occur if the needs are met? What will be different—and how?
Where are they? (General: city/state; and specific: neighborhood, geography)	What is the problem? (Get specific)		How is the problem linked to your organization?
When is the problem evident?			

Problem Statement Review Questions

Once a problem statement is completed, answer the following six questions to see whether what has been developed hits the mark:

1. Is the problem statement focused on those who will be served by the program (and not on your organization)?

2. Does the problem statement directly connect to the organization's mission statement?

3. Given the organization's size and resources, can it address the problem in a meaningful way?

4. Is the problem statement adequately supported by solid and reputable quantitative and qualitative data on the nature, size, and scope of the need to be addressed?

5. Is it sweet and simple (remember KISS from a previous chapter)?

6. Is the problem statement persuasive without being wordy?

Reality Check

Avoid the trap of circular reasoning, which commonly occurs in problem statements. To use the Foundation Center's definition and example, circular reasoning occurs when "you present the absence of your solution as the actual problem. Then your solution is offered as the way to solve the problem. For example, 'The problem is that we have no pool in our community. Building a pool will solve the problem.'"

This statement does not communicate a problem: communities across the country thrive with no community pool. However, if it was stated that a community pool in the neighborhood would specifically address certain challenges the community is facing, and if followed up by citing a similar community where a community pool has had a positive impact in ways that are documented, it could potentially build a compelling argument that would provide the context for the problem statement.

The program's need is now established. Developing the program's goals and objectives is next, which is Step Four.

Step 4
Defining Clear Goals and Objectives

IN THIS STEP GRANTSEEKERS LEARN the concept of writing clear goals and objectives. Grantseekers must also focus on the important differences between them. Using a worksheet and following the examples, grantseekers construct goals and a set of objectives for their own proposals.

Purpose of the Goals and Objectives Components: The "So What?" Factor

Once the problem to be addressed by an organization is identified and clearly articulated via the problem statement, the next step is to develop solid goals that clearly define what the organization intends to accomplish through its program and also to establish measurable objectives that will indicate the organization's progress toward its goals. The goals and objectives will allow the organization and its funders to know whether the program is successful at the conclusion of the grant. Poorly defined goals and objectives, or goals without objectives, push projects into missed milestones, overworked staff, unhappy clients, and disillusioned funders. Goals and objectives should be clear statements of purpose that define the end result of the project.[1]

Definition of Goals and Objectives

Words can be confusing, especially if the assumption is made that everyone understands what they mean. For this reason, let's clarify one more time: A goal is what the program aspires to achieve and the objectives are how an organization will know if it is meeting its goal(s). This distinction is the foundation upon which successful goals and objectives are based. Equally important is the fact that both goals and objectives are directly tied to the problem statement (Step Three). Also, each goal will have one or more objectives. However, it is worthwhile to note that smaller projects may have only one focused goal and two or three objectives.

Definitions

Goals. "Goals are things your organization hopes to achieve. Goals can be set at the organizational level, the program level, and the individual employee level."[2]

  Example: Youth in underserved communities in King County who complete the Swim 4 Life program will know how to swim.

Objectives. "Objectives are smaller steps that one must accomplish to reach a goal, and they're always stated in a way that can be measured."[3]

  Example: In the Learn-to-Swim program within one year:

- 100 percent of participants will recognize the rules of water safety

- 90 percent of participants will demonstrate basic water safety and drowning prevention skills

- 80 percent of participants will develop self-confidence as swimmers and the motivation to improve physical fitness

---

Everyone struggles in the beginning with the difference between goals and objectives. Use the following side-by-side comparison as an aid.[4]

Goals	Objectives
Are broad statements	Are realistic steps to achieve the goal(s)
Provide focus, vision, and direction	Are always active and use strong action verbs
Can be idealistic and do not necessarily have to be reached during the proposed grant period	Answer: What? Why? Who? How? When?
	Can be validated
Can be nonspecific and nonmeasureable	Are clear to everyone with a basic knowledge
	Are SMART:
	Specific
	Measurable
	Achievable
	Relevant
	Time-bound

Example of Strong Goals and Objectives

Goals	Objectives
Our theater is enjoyed by all our communities	Fifty percent of our Asian/Pacific Islander audience will increase their attendance from one show per year to two shows by end of the year.
There is a playground within walking distance for all children	Increase the access to playgrounds for children in Eastown by two playgrounds each year for the next five years.
Asthma is no longer the number one reason that children miss school	All students in grades K–3 who are diagnosed with asthma decrease their incidents of severe attacks by 15 percent in the first semester.
All adults can read confidently to their children	Eighty-five percent of first-time, new parents in the Barrisville section of Anytown can read and have child-appropriate books in their homes within a year of their first child's birth.

Outcome Focus Objectives

It is important to ensure that a grant proposal's objectives focus on outcomes (the change) versus the process (how the change will be made). The "how" is addressed in the next step, which focuses on methods (also referred to as strategies). When the focus is on outcomes, the focus is on the results of an organization's actions. It is important to be able to envision what will be different because of the actions of the organization. What is the organization hoping to accomplish? What will be different, improved, better? What can be measured?

An example of an outcome objective: In the next year, a minimum of eighty new parents who complete the program will increase their confidence in their role as disciplinarian and teacher as evidenced by achieving at least a 90 percent on their final parenting quiz.

Process objectives focus on activities. By focusing on the outcomes instead of the process, it allows an organization the flexibility needed to reach its intended results. An organization can adjust and edit the methods when needed and as needed to reach its objectives, a process that leads ultimately to achieving its goals. An example of a process objective: To recruit 120 parents for our parent education courses.

Definitions

Methods, also known as *strategies* or *tactics,* are the activities that an organization will use to deliver its services in order to reach its objectives. When working on a proposal, the focus begins on the goals. The order is as follows:

1. *Goal* is what the program will achieve. Goals are visionary and may not be measurable.

2. *Objectives* are how grantseekers will know if their program is meeting its goal(s). Objectives are measurable.

3. *Methods* define the strategies or activities needed to accomplish the objectives. Methods are the "how to."

Because outcomes are considered powerful indicators of success, this workbook focuses more specifically on these objectives rather than process objectives. More and more funders, as well as individual donors, are looking to make an impact or positive change with their grants. A grantseeker's outcome objectives as outlined in their proposal will assist funders in understanding how their investment in the organization will make a difference or impact.

Reality Check: Advocacy

Creating systems change, advocating for a community, group of people or position, and/or community activism takes time and the path to success is not always clear or easy to quantify. Thus, because of the nature of this kind of work, it is important to include outcome objectives as well as process objectives. These process objectives are the small wins that allow everyone to measure the progress in moving toward the goals.

Example for Advocacy Work

- Outcome: Schools remove all vending machines from campus.
- Process or small win: Have a proposition on the November ballot banning vending machines in schools.
- Process or small win: Collect enough signatures to be on the November ballot.

The following chart contains some questions that may help grantseekers define better outcomes.[5]

Process-Oriented Questions	Outcome-Oriented Questions
What services do you offer?	What community results do you hope to accomplish through your services?
What is it that your organization does?	What is it that your organization is striving to achieve?
Describe the service needs your agency meets?	What change in condition or behavior are you attempting to effect in the people you serve?

Writing Outcome Objectives

Answering the following questions will help in clearly articulating the results the organization expects to accomplish:

- Based on the problem statement, what is (are) the key area(s) the organization is seeking to change?

- Who (what segment of the population or community) will be involved in the change?

- How will the change be measured (an increase or improvement, or a decrease and reduction)? And by what degree (by how much)?

- When will this change take place? How many months or years or by what specific date?

- After you have written your objectives, it is helpful to run one last test to see if the objectives are "SMART":[6]

  - Specific: Do they clearly explain what the change the organization wants will be? Are they action oriented?

  - Measurable: Do the objectives help everyone know precisely when the goal(s) have been reached?

  - Achievable: This is the reality check. Based on available resources (knowledge, funding, staffing, partners, physical space, etc.) and access to the target population, will the organization be able to make the change it envisions within the defined time? And with the resources requested? It is important to strike a balance between being overly ambitious and aiming too low.

  - Relevant: Are the objectives results-oriented and rewarding to the organization, its funder(s), and, most important, the community being served?

  - Time-bound: What is the deadline for reaching the change envisioned? Is it tangible and tractable?

> ## Helpful Hint
>
> *Objectives measure* an increase or improvement, or a decrease and reduction. Therefore, use phrases like the following examples to assist in framing organizational outcome objectives appropriately:
>
> To reduce   To increase
>
> To decrease   To expand

Tips for Writing Good Goals and Objectives

Do . . .

- Include at least one focused goal for the project and one or two outcome objectives.

- Make sure that the goals and objectives tie back to the problem statement. This is critical.

- Include all relevant groups in the target population in the goal(s). Although when writing objectives, consider specifying an outcome for a specific population or community.

- Allow plenty of time to accomplish objectives. Things always take longer to implement than planned. It is better to undercommit and overperform than to overcommit and underperform.

Don't . . .

- Overly commit what can be accomplished. Limit the number of goals to one to three per program and no more than three objectives per goal. The reason is this: an organization will need to keep track of all the objectives and methods tied to the goals, so the entire process needs to be manageable.

- Confuse outcome objectives and methods or activities. Collaborating with the YMCA to expand the program and keep costs low is a method. Expanding the Swim 4 Life program to the Cooperville Elementary School resulting in an additional 100 kids completing the program over the course of 2012 is an outcome objective, as it describes the result achieved through the intervention outlined in the method.

- Forget to budget for evaluation activities (Step Six) if measuring the objective(s) will have costs associated with them.

Use Worksheet 4.1A to prepare to write proposal goals and objectives by focusing on outcomes. Start by writing down the goal of the program. Then describe the objectives that tie to that goal. Use the filled-out Worksheet 4.1B as a guide. If an organization has more than one goal for its program, use a separate copy of Worksheet 4.1A for each goal. Limit the objectives to no more than three per goal.

WORKSHEET 4.1A:
Goals and Objectives Exercise

On the Web

Worksheet 4.1B contains sample goals and objectives based on the Swim 4 Life Program. Grantseekers should refer to it as they complete this worksheet for themselves.

GOAL:

	Objective 1	Objective 2	Objective 3	Objective 4
Direction of change				
Area of change				
Target population				
Degree of change				
Time frame				

Follow this standard form as objective statements are developed: To (direction of change) + (area of change) + (target population) + (degree of change) + (time frame).

WORKSHEET 4.1B:
Objective Worksheet Completed for the Swim 4 Life Program

GOAL: All youth in underserved communities in the Gathenton School District will know how to swim and understand the rules of water safety.

	Objective 1	Objective 2	Objective 3	Objective 4
Direction of change	Increase			
Area of change	Underserved youth in the Gathenton School District			
Target population	Students at Cooperville Middle School in Abbington			
Degree of change	25% increase in student participation over previous year			
Time frame	One full school year			

When this is completed, go through the Goals and Objectives Review Questions with the same approach as the problem statement. Remember, the goal is to be able to answer yes to each question in the review questions.

Goals and Objectives Review Questions

1. Are the goals stated as results? And do they relate to the problem statement?

2. Are the outcome objectives stated as specific results that relate to a program goal? Are they steppingstones to achieving success (the goal)? Can everyone understand them?

3. Can progress in meeting the objectives be measured and assessed?

4. Do the objectives describe the population and a specific time frame for change?

The organization's problem statement is in order, and the "so what?" factor has been specifically addressed in the program's goals and objectives. So let's move on to Step Five where the development of the organization's methods, or activities, will help in achieving the program's objectives, thus leading to the accomplishment of the program's goals.

Notes

1. Rhonda Goetz. January 2010. Defining Project Goals and Objectives. www.projectsmart.co.uk

2. Stan Hutton and Frances Phillips. 2001. *Nonprofit Kit for Dummies*. Hoboken, NJ: Wiley, p. 131.

3. Stan Hutton and Frances Phillips. 2001. *Nonprofit Kit for Dummies*. Hoboken, NJ: Wiley, p. 131.

4. Adapted from UCLA Center for Health Policy Research. Health Data, Train the Trainer Project. Performing a Community Assessment Curriculum. 2004. www.healthpolicy.ucla.edu/healthdata/tw_cba4.pdf

5. Adapted from Robert A. Penna and William J. Phillips. 2004. *Outcome Frameworks*. Rensselaerville Institute's Center for Outcomes. Albany, NY: Fort Orange Press, p. 8.

6. Paul J. Meyer. 2003. "What Would You Do If You Knew You Couldn't Fail? Creating S.M.A.R.T. Goals." *Attitude Is Everything: If You Want to Succeed Above and Beyond*. Meyer Resource Group, Inc. www.pauljmeyer.com

Step 5
Developing the Methods

THE METHODS AN ORGANIZATION USES to reach its objectives are the focus of this step. Grantseekers look at the elements of the methods component of a proposal and learn how to use a time line to more easily see what will happen. Using a worksheet and examples, organizations can write their methods for the objectives developed in Step Four.

Purpose of the Methods Component

The problem statement is clearly articulated, and the goals and objectives are set. The methods component of the proposal systematically walks funders through the strategies the organization proposes to carry out in order to accomplish its objectives. Methods answer this key question: how will an organization actually accomplish its work?

Content of the Methods Component

Methods—also frequently referred to as strategies—are detailed descriptions of the activities an organization will implement to achieve the ends specified in its objectives. However they are referred to, this section of the proposal should clearly spell out the methods to be used and give the reasons for choosing them. Any research supporting the use of these methods—such as their previous success or, if the methods are untested, data that support the assertion that these methods might prove successful—should be included. This section should also address whether the methods selected are already in place within the organization and simply being replicated by the program, or whether they are new. Finally, this section should describe who will staff the program and their qualifications, and identify the client population to be served, along with a justification of why this population was selected.

To develop the methods component, answer the following questions:

1. What are the elements that are inflexible (such as date of completion, dollars available, staffing needed)?

2. What activities need to be carried out in order to meet the objectives?

3. What are the starting and ending dates of these activities?

4. Who has responsibility for completing each activity?

5. How will participants be selected? (This question is not applicable to all projects.)

6. How was this methodology determined to be the best one to solve the problem presented? Does it build on models already in existence, or is it a different approach? If it is different, why is it different? And why did the organization select it?

The methods section should be realistic—the organization should be able to complete the proposed activities within the time frame stated in the proposal using the available resources. For proposals with multiple objectives and methods, it is a good idea to include a timeline showing when each method will start and finish. The accompanying Sample Timeline for the Swim 4 Life Program shows one way to chart a nonprofit's activities on a timeline.

Tips for Writing the Methods Component

- Align the organization's methods to the program's objectives and problem statement.

- Tie the methods to the resources being requested in the program budget. Each activity should match its corresponding cost exactly.

- Explain the rationale for choosing these methods; talk in terms of research findings, best practices, expert opinion, and the organization's past experience with similar programs.

- Spell out the facilities and capital equipment that will be available for the project.

- Build various activity phases on top of one another to move the effort toward the desired results. Include a timeline.

- Be sure to discuss who will be served and how they will be chosen.

- Do not assume that the funder knows about the nonprofit, its target audience, or what it proposes to accomplish.

Sample Timeline (Abbreviated Version)

Activity	Month	1	2	3	4	5	6
Contact the point person at Cooperville and set up planning meeting.		X					
Hold first meeting with point person at Cooperville, the PE teacher, and a representative of the PTA.			X				
Hold follow-up meeting with the point person at Cooperville and the point person at Rockmore to coordinate pool usage.			X				
Create recruitment materials for new site.		X					
Update all recruitment materials to incorporate Cooperville.			X				
Develop and finalize the specific outreach strategies for all sites that specifically incorporate Cooperville.				X			
Schedule an Interested Parents meeting and student assembly at Cooperville and recruit/confirm at least five parents from the other two schools to provide testimonials for both programs.				X			
Finalize the evaluation tools for the Cooperville site.				X			
Recruit a minimum of 25 students for the program.					X		
Officially launch the project at Cooperville with a public event that will feature Jane Swimmer, program founder and hometown hero, as well as Tia Jones, program manager.							X
Evaluate and document progress at the new site.				X	X	X	X

Look over the Sample Methods Component for the Swim 4 Life program. Then develop the organization's methods by completing Worksheet 5.1, which should list the key elements of the organization's planned program. Finally, use the Methods Review Questions to review the organization's methods in the same way the questions were deployed in the organization's program statement and goals and objectives.

Sample Methods Component

Our primary objective in 2013 for the Swim 4 Life Program will employ the methods as outlined below. These methods have been proven successful as they are the same methods we used to launch our program at our current two school sites: Arthur Schomburg Middle School and the Rockmore Education Complex High School. It should be noted that Cooperville Middle School is located in Abbington, where Rockmore is also located, and we fully intend to leverage the relationships we've already established.

OBJECTIVE
To increase the swimming competence and confidence of the underserved youth in the Gathenton School District by adding Cooperville Middle School and increasing overall student participation by 25 percent within one full school year.

METHODS
- Swim 4 Life program manager will recruit a point person on staff at Cooperville who has a specific interest in the program.
- The Cooperville point person will work in collaboration with the program manager to
  - Create a small task force inclusive of the physical education teacher and a representative of the PTA
  - Hold a short series of meetings with the program manager, the Cooperville task force, and a point person from the Rockmore task force to share best practices, lay out the recruitment plan, agree on the evaluation plan and specific benchmarks, and coordinate schedules for the use of the pools
  - Create specific recruitment materials for the Cooperville site and update the general program materials to incorporate Cooperville as a new site
  - Host an Interested Parents meeting and separate Interested Students assembly at Cooperville, making sure we recruit and confirm at least five parents and students from the two other program sites to provide testimonials about the program at the meeting and assembly
  - Launch a time specific recruitment period targeting a minimum of twenty-five kids
- Once officially launched, the program manager will formally chart the progress of each participant, noting the specific benchmarks along the way as established in the evaluation.

WORKSHEET 5.1:
Methods Exercise

On the Web

Task and Subtasks	Person(s) Responsible	Resources Needed	Start and Finish Dates

Methods Review Questions

1. Do the methods discussed in the proposal derive logically from the problem statement and the goals and objectives?

2. Do the methods present the program activities to be undertaken?

3. Has the grantseeker explained why they selected the specific methods or activities?

4. Has the grantseeker explained the timing and order of the specific activities?

5. Is it clear who will perform specific activities? And do their credentials and/or experience demonstrate that they are appropriate to carry out the activities of the program?

6. Given the organization's projected resources, are the proposed activities feasible?

If an organization is following along with each step, including testing each proposal component against the questions at the end of each, it is now in prime position to be successful in the next step: developing the evaluation component, which is Step Six.

Step 6
Preparing the Evaluation Component

EVERYTHING COMPLETED UP TO THIS POINT in the development of the organization's proposal (problem statement, goals, objectives, and methods) naturally leads to this component, as evaluation answers critical questions that both the organization and the funder have, such as

- Was the program successful?
- Did it do what it was designed to do?
- What impact did the program have on the community or target population?
- What did the organization learn from this experience that can be leveraged?
- What didn't work—and why or why not?
- What's different in the community or the lives of those targeted as a result of the program?

Just as the preparation of the goals, objectives, and methods required clarity, focus, and strategy, it is now more important than ever to plan how the organization will evaluate what it proposes to do. This step explores learning how to write an authentic and effective evaluation plan so that the organization can effectively demonstrate the success of its program and measure program impact—and also capture the lessons learned. An exercise will help grantseekers think about what their evaluation plans should contain.

Definitions

Impact. "The fundamental intended or unintended long-term change occurring in organizations, communities, or systems as a result of program activities."

Leverage. "A method of grantmaking practiced by some foundations. Leverage occurs when a small amount of money is given with the express purpose of attracting funding from other sources or of providing the organization with the tools it needs to raise other kinds of funds. Leverage may also be defined as building momentum from one effort to the next."

Purpose of the Evaluation Component

Evaluation is a process that determines the impact, effectiveness, and efficiency of a program. It reveals what worked and—equally important—what did not. Decisions made during this process can help the organization plan for the program's future, and the process can produce an organized and objective report documenting the return on investment for funders and the realized benefits to the community the organization serves. How a program will be evaluated must be determined prior to implementation so that the organization can build evaluation measurements into the final program plan—before the program or its expansion is launched. Always keep in mind that funders expect to hear from organizations how they define and measure the success of a program, whether they explicitly request an evaluation or not.

Definition

Return on Investment (ROI). "The amount of benefit (return) based on the amount of resources (funds) used to produce it."

Specific Virtues of Evaluation

First, a good evaluation component strengthens the proposal from the funder's perspective. Grantseekers are asking potential grantmakers to invest in their organization and program—and they are asking the funding staff to be their advocate. They want the funder to bet on the fact that the world as the nonprofit sees it will be improved in some specific way as a result of the proposed program. Essentially, proposed programs serve to test a hypothesis: "If we do this, then that will happen." A solid evaluation component in a proposal reassures a funder that the organization is interested, as the funder is, in learning whether this hypothesis is correct.

Second, through evaluation, the organization will learn about the program's strengths and areas of weakness. The process alone of thinking through the evaluation design can strengthen a program before it's even implemented. From there, the organization can take the knowledge gained through an actual evaluation and share it with staff and volunteers to improve programs as they are being implemented. This knowledge may also be shared with others in the field so that they, too, can learn the lessons of the program's work.

The third benefit is to the public—the impact. Dollars granted from foundations and corporate giving programs are dollars dedicated to charitable good; therefore, with each grant an organization receives, it becomes a recipient of public trust once again. Because of that, the organization has an obligation to ensure that its programs are actually having a positive impact on the community as a whole or on the target audience that it purports to serve within the community. Evaluation is one of the strongest and most effective tools any nonprofit has to verify and document that it is indeed fulfilling its obligation to make a positive impact on the community it serves.

Definition

Hypothesis. "The assumed proposition that is tested in a research process."

Internal or External Evaluation

Some foundations will allow organizations to designate from 5 to 10 percent (sometimes more) of the total program budget for evaluation; others will not. Therefore, organizations need to consider how they will evaluate their programs for the purpose of documenting results, key findings, and lessons learned. There are some organizations that will spend time up front, crystallizing their evaluation components and coming to feel confident that they have both the staffing and the expertise in place to objectively and thoroughly handle the evaluation internally. Other organizations will decide to engage an outside evaluator, for any number of reasons, such as (1) lacking expertise among the staff, (2) having the staff expertise but lacking the staff time to dedicate to evaluation, or (3) wanting the evaluation to be deemed as objective as possible. These are three of the most common reasons for hiring an outside evaluator. In any case, organizations should provide some background information in the proposal that indicates which direction it intends to take. The proposal budget should also reflect an expense line item for evaluation.

Content of the Evaluation Component

The ability to fully understand both the big picture of the program and the individual pieces that make up that big picture is a must. Evaluation design requires dedicated thinking. First, one needs to consider the organization's definition of success—the "so what?" factor. Then one must determine the relationship between the expected outcomes and the activities described in the proposal. Finally, one needs to identify the most important aspects of the program, then identify why it is important to evaluate them.

Organizations conduct evaluations primarily to accomplish six specific goals:

1. Find out whether or not the hypothesis was correct: Did what the organization originally propose actually do what the organization expected that it would?

2. Determine whether the methods that were specified were indeed used and the objectives met.

3. Determine whether an impact was made on the problem identified.

4. Obtain feedback from the clients served and other members of the community.

5. Maintain some control over the project.

6. Make midcourse corrections along the way to increase the program's chances of success.

When preparing the evaluation section of the proposal, answering the following questions will help to frame what will be stated:

1. What is the specific purpose of the organization's evaluation?

2. How will the findings be used?

3. What will the organization know after the evaluation that it does not know now?

4. What will the organization do after the evaluation that it cannot do now because of lack of information?

5. How will the lives of the people or community served by the organization be better?

6. Did the organization use the funder's investment wisely? Were the funds effectively managed or leveraged?

7. Was the program budget accurate?

Unlike previous editions of this workbook, the accompanying website creates the platform to provide a plethora of information on program evaluation. Within the confines of the actual workbook, a broad overview is provided that can be of some assistance as grantseekers determine the parameters most appropriate for the program. Generally, there are two approaches to data collection: quantitative methods and qualitative methods.

Quantitative methods are, as the name implies, methods to quantify (measure or count) data. Using this method, data are collected that can be analyzed statistically, via averages, means, percentiles, and the like. According to the Nonprofit Good Practice Guide Glossary (www.npgoodpractice .org/Glossary), this approach "involves the use of numerical measurement and data analysis based on statistical methods. It is an assessment process that answers the question, 'How much did we do?'" These analyses allow organizations to make statements about cause-and-effect relationships. Employ quantitative methods for questions focused on

- Understanding the quantities or frequency of particular aspects of a program (such as number of enrollees or number of dropouts)

- Determining whether a cause-and-effect relationship is present

- Comparing two different methods seeking to achieve the same outcomes

- Establishing numerical baselines (through such means as pretests, posttests, and quarterly or yearly follow-ups)

Qualitative methods, in contrast, are based on direct contact with the people involved with a program. These methods consist of interviews (group or individual), observation (direct or field), and personal stories told both in writing and in photo or video, as well as review of selected documents. According to the Nonprofit Good Practice Guide Glossary (www .npgoodpractice.org/Glossary), this approach is "mainly concerned with the properties, the state, and the character (i.e., the nature) of phenomena. It implies an emphasis on processes and meanings that are rigorously examined, but not measured in terms of quantity, amount, or frequency." Employ qualitative methods for questions focused on

- Understanding feelings or opinions about a program among participants, staff, or community members

- Gaining insight into how patterns of relationships in the program unfold

- Gathering multiple perspectives to understand the whole picture

- Identifying approximate indicators that clients are moving in the "right" direction

In other words, pretests and posttests are not the only measures of success. By taking the time up front to think clearly and strategically, an organization can come up with a creative and valuable evaluation design that incorporates both quantitative and qualitative methods.

Take a look at the Sample Evaluation Component prepared for the Swim 4 Life program:

Sample Evaluation Component

Evaluation of age groups at RLC and after-school programs at Arthur Schomberg and Cooperville will offer opportunities to measure long-term outcomes. Staff will measure student performance by improvement in times for each stroke at various distances. Medical professionals from Any City University Hospital and educators from Some City College and Everytown University will assist in formulating an evaluation construct measuring changes in physical fitness (flexibility, aerobic endurance, and weight) and academic performance (attendance, drop-out rates, grades, and interest in going to college). Resulting data will be disseminated to the school administrators and district, reported to other stakeholders—including the XYZ Foundation if this request is approved—and used to continually improve the program. Expected long-term outcomes include increased scores on state mandated fitness tests performed in students' physical education classes.

To evaluate the overall effectiveness of the Swim 4 Life program at its three sites, we will have our instructors use pretest and posttest assessments, in addition to direct observation of students in the water so that baseline performance can be determined for all participants. Children's progress in the Learn-to-Swim Program is evaluated based on effort made and skills achieved as evidenced by participants holding their breath under water, ability to dog paddle from the middle of the pool to the side of the pool, and ability to tread water for a minimum of one minute. The assessment process also tracks changes in attitude toward swimming as evidenced by qualitative written storytelling from a minimum of 25 percent of program participants. In addition, instructors will administer a multiple-choice exam on water safety at the end of each four-week session. After the first six months of program implementation, the goal is to have participants answer an average of 75 percent of the questions correctly. School administrators, teachers, and parents will be sought for qualitative feedback on a scale of 1–100 percent relative to their satisfaction with the program and to influence its implementation strategies, administrative processes, and related activities. For those students with IEPs, we will conduct a parent satisfaction survey with the goal of showing a minimum 85 percent favorability rating of the program.

Answer the questions in Worksheet 6.1 to begin planning the evaluation section. When completing the evaluation section, review it with the Evaluation Review Questions.

WORKSHEET 6.1:
Evaluation Planning Questionnaire

1. What questions will the organization's evaluation activities seek to answer?

2. What are the specific evaluation plans and time frames?

    a. What kinds of data will be collected?

    b. At what points?

    c. Using what strategies or instruments?

    d. Using what comparison group or baseline, if any?

3. If the intention is to study a sample of participants, how will this sample be constructed?

WORKSHEET 6.1:
Evaluation Planning Questionnaire (Continued)

4. What procedures will be used to determine whether the program was implemented as planned?

5. Who will conduct the evaluation?

6. Who will receive the results?

7. How is success being defined for this program or project?

Evaluation Review Questions

1. Does the evaluation section focus on assessing the project results?

2. Does it describe how the evaluation will assess the efficiency of program methods?

3. Does it describe who will be evaluated and what will be measured?

4. Does it state what information will be collected in the evaluation process?

5. Does it state who will be responsible for making the assessments?

6. Does it discuss how the information and conclusions will be used to improve the program?

7. Does it provide the organization's definition of success?

If the program is successful and the organization is able to document that success through evaluation, it is probably going to want that program to continue. Step Seven addresses the need to plan now for program sustainability beyond the initial funding.

Step 7
Developing Sustainability Strategies

IN THIS STEP GRANTSEEKERS LEARN how to develop strategies to continue the program beyond the initial grant funding. Other resources, and other funding strategies, are potentially available to keep programs running, but the organization must position itself early to take full advantage of—that is, to leverage—the first grant(s). Grantseekers identify, through exercises and examples, the potential sources of ongoing support that are best for the program.

Purpose of the Sustainability Component

The purpose of this component is to help grantseekers consider how the program will be funded past its immediate future—to begin with the end in mind, so-to-speak. Potential funders want to know that organizations are thinking beyond their funding; they want assurance that the organization is planning beyond the scope of their time-limited funding. How will the organization continue the good work upon which the community has come to depend? The old saying "last but not least" applies well here: this might be the last section of narrative in the proposal, but it is by no means the least important.

Content of the Sustainability Component

The sustainability component needs to reflect whether the proposal is seeking program, capital or equipment, or capacity-building funding. Then it must address how the program will continue once the grant comes to a close. When a program ends prematurely, it typically leaves unfinished business. In other words, it fails to achieve its intended goals and therefore does not successfully address the need outlined at the beginning of the proposal. *And let's not forget the ultimate impact that this has on the clients, constituents, and community who come to rely on the program or service.* For that reason, funders pay much more attention to this section than most grantseekers would probably suspect because they will have a vested interest in the project's success *beyond their funding.* Therefore, this section of the proposal should provide a framework that shows how the nonprofit plans to continue the program beyond the funder's investment, as well as who on the organization's staff will be responsible for making this plan happen.

In capital or equipment proposals (major equipment purchases or building renovations and expansion) funders will want to know what the associated costs are for operating the new equipment, for maintaining the new building, or for increasing services if building expansion results in program expansion. They will want this information because these are all costs that the organization will incur beyond the funding being requested. Organizations will also need to show that the sources of funding meet these additional costs.

In the case of a capacity-building grant, funders want to know how the nonprofit will support the capacity it has grown. For example, a request might be made for a capacity-building grant to increase the organization's fundraising ability via the creation of a development plan. Once the plan is created—and the grant is expended—how does the organization plan to pay for the actual implementation of the new development plan?

Consider future funding from one or more of these sources:

- *Continuation grants from foundations and corporations.* A nonprofit can seek continuing support from those foundations and corporations that fund ongoing programs. However, as was stated earlier, many funders prefer to support new and expanding programs—not continuation funding for existing programs. A bright spot is that there are also funders who, if cultivated and stewarded properly, will continue to support organizations beyond their initial investment. Once again, both the funder research along with the relationship building, as outlined in Step Two, have a direct impact on the outcome of continuation funding.

- *Fees for service.* If a nonprofit opts to ask clients to pay fees, the fee scale and a revenue plan should be shown in the proposal.

- *Sales of items or activities.* A nonprofit might be able to set up an income-producing situation, such as a gift shop or thrift store. In addition, it might be able to sell publications, concert recordings, or educational activities. Revenues generated from these sales might cover some costs of the program. If this route is taken, a clear expense and revenue projection should be a part of the proposal. (*Please note:* Organizations need to check with both legal counsel and accounting counsel to ensure that any revenue-generating ventures launched are set up and monitored in accordance with IRS guidelines.)

A typical mistake that grantseekers make in their proposals is not taking this component as seriously as they should and not fully understanding that grant funding does in fact come to an end. Saying something to the effect of "future funding will come from a mix of sources such as other grants and individual support" is not a sustainability plan.

Tips for Writing the Sustainability Component

Helpful Hint

Toot your own horn! If an organization has examples to share of other instances in which it successfully continued programs beyond initial funding, this would be the place to share such information, because it speaks to the organization's credibility not only in launching programs but also in maintaining them.

Many funders ask specifically for this component in their grant guidelines; others do not. Whether or not this component is required, grantseekers should include some information on sources of support for the project's future.

The more specific grantseekers are in this section, the more confidence they will inspire in potential funders that the project will continue beyond their grant, thereby maximizing the impact of their investment.

Take a look at the Sample Sustainability Component to see what the Swim 4 Life has planned for the sustainability of its program.

Sample Sustainability Component

Our model is built to be self-sustaining. Swim 4 Life's overhead is extremely low (10 percent), since we leverage the resources of the Gathentown School District by using its pools and our program's target audience is its school children. The Swim 4 Life partnership with both the YWCA of Greater King County, Any State, as well as the Some City School Program, further leverage resources already available and with a track record of over a decade each of financial stability. Both programs have indicated a desire to enter into a long-term agreement with Swim 4 Life, pending our ability to scale up to meet the needs of more kids. Finally, we hired a half-time development director in June 2010 and increased her to full-time status in June 2011 after seeing our revenue from individuals increase from zero to $60,000 in one year.

The programs currently offered by the Swim 4 Life program are expected to be the first of many throughout King County, Any State, as the county continues to seek partnerships with our program in collaboration with other larger, established social service organizations. There are additional schools in parts of the city that have underused swim facilities and that lack safe and accessible programs; we believe strongly in our model and our ability to bring it to scale throughout the Gathentown School District. In response to numerous requests, the program staff are now pursuing Learn-to-Swim classes for teachers and other classified district personnel targeted for 2013, which would create a new revenue stream to support the children's programs. In addition, this would help fulfill the mission to empower youth by creating bonding experiences with teachers who model healthy activities.

The partnership with the Gathentown School District offers the Swim 4 Life program the opportunity to outreach to students in some of the most underserved communities in King County—those who are most in need of the benefits of structured and supervised physical activity—while keeping operating costs low. Since the district provides the pool facilities and program participants, the Swim 4 Life program is liable only for the wages of instructors and lifeguards, thus resulting in an exceptionally cost-effective model.

Answering the questions in Worksheet 7.1 will assist in starting to develop the future funding component of your proposal. Be sure to check the work by answering the Sustainability Review Questions.

WORKSHEET 7.1:
Future Funding Questionnaire

Risks and Opportunities	Sources of Future Financial Resources	Internal Requirements
Do we intend to continue this project?	What sources can we use?	What internal plans do we have for obtaining future funding?
For how long?		
What resources (direct and indirect) are needed?		

Sustainability Review Questions

1. Is it the organization's intent to have the program continue after the initial grant funding is gone?

2. If yes, does the sustainability component of the proposal present a plan for securing future funding for the program?

3. Does it discuss future funding strategies or earned-income strategies?

4. If the organization is requesting a multiyear grant, did it show that the organization will have a decreasing reliance on grant support each year? (Grantmakers are more inclined to make a multiyear grant to nonprofits that assume greater financial responsibility for the project each year, rather than asking the funder to maintain the same level of funding each year.)

It is now time to develop the budget using Step Eight.

Step 8
Developing the Program Budget

THIS STEP PROVIDES THE BASIC TOOLS to develop an effective program budget. It also introduces key terms and definitions that will help in understanding the various elements of a budget. Finally, there are a number of examples and tools included both here and online that will be helpful in creating a program budget.

General Budget Overview

When applying for grants typically two types of budgets may be requested—an organizational *operating* budget and a *program* budget.

An organizational operating budget details the income and expenses for the fiscal year for the grantseeking organization. An organization may have several projects or programs that it is responsible for implementing and managing throughout the year. A program budget would essentially fall under the purview of the organizational operating budget.

The program budget is one of the most important components of a grant proposal. It provides insight into how a single program plan will be financially executed during the life of the grant or program. The budget also gives funders the opportunity to understand the depth and breadth of the programmatic effort from a financial perspective. One of the first things that funders want to know is what the budget entails and how its money will make an impact if it funds the program or organization. While many organizations have the skills to implement the program plan, it may not necessarily know how to financially explain or manage its program.

Helpful Hint

Be sure to research what an acceptable indirect cost rate should be. Some funders have already established their allowable indirect cost rate for any grants they fund. For instance, if a funder will only allow an indirect cost rate of 12 percent, but the organization's indirect cost rate is 20 percent, the program will have to off-set the 8 percent loss in overhead costs in other areas of the budget.

For the purpose of this workbook, only the *program budget* will be specifically addressed.

Basics of a Program Budget

Developing a budget for a grant proposal can be somewhat similar to developing a personal budget. For instance, while personal expenses might include mortgage or rent, utility bills and personal loans, the program budget includes expenses such as salaries, marketing, and other cost items necessary to successfully run the program.

The following is a list of simple stages that are necessary to develop a program budget.

Stage 1: Review, research, and organize budget requirements and information

Stage 2: Develop and document the program budget

Stage 3: Review, update, and review again

Stage 4: Develop the budget justification

Incorporating these specific stages into a budget development process will ensure a comprehensive budget that is reflective of thoughtfulness and planning. Funders will pay close attention to a grantseeker's efforts to adhere to their budget requirements, document projected revenues, and research relevant expenses for their proposed program.

Stage 1: Review, Research, and Organize

The first stage is a two-part process that starts the budget formulation process. The first part involves reading the grant application for understanding and clarity, while the second part demonstrates how to research and organize the information to be included in the budget. Let's begin by understanding the grant application budget review process.

Review the Grant Application for Specific Budget Requirements

Before investing too much time in developing the budget and selecting a budget tool, it is important to read through the grant application and determine what is required. Funders often provide or specify a document or tool that should be used to capture the budget, as well as identify or list specific information to be included. As a potential grantee, it is important to follow the specific instructions provided in the grant application, supplementing it with any information (if allowed by the funder) that will make the organization's financial needs more clear.

Important items to consider in the grant application guidelines before developing the budget may include

- A budget template with instructions including whether or not it is mandatory to use the form

- Instructions on the specific budget categories or level of the budget details and how those details should be recorded

- Items that should not be included in the budget

- If a *budget narrative* should be included and in what format

- Clarity around the percentage of "indirect" or "overhead" an organization is allowed to include in the budget. This will vary greatly from funder to funder, as well as for public funding at the local, state, and federal levels.

While this stage might appear tedious for some, it is absolutely necessary to get a funder's attention, as well as to demonstrate an organization's understanding of the importance of having its financial house in order. By following directions, an organization further demonstrates its level of commitment to its program.

Now that the budget instructions and specific requirements have been properly read and digested, it's time to begin researching and organizing specific budget details.

Research and Organize Budget Information

The process of researching, collecting, and organizing the budget data is often underestimated when developing the budget. What if an organization has never used the services of a printer for printing marketing material? How does the organization know how much it will cost to perform that task? This stage demonstrates the process to collect the information required to determine revenue and expense estimates that will be included in the budget.

Before actually beginning to develop the budget, there are several actions that should occur:

- Identifying the types of revenues and expenses that are included in the organization's budget

- Researching, developing, or collecting estimates for revenues and expenses

---

Helpful Hint

Using a spreadsheet to document the information researched will help to track and organize the information collected.

- Organizing the data to easily facilitate the budget development process (next step)

- Remembering that budgets consist of good faith estimates—a best guess based on solid research.

Thinking that perhaps this process is time consuming? That would be a correct assumption. It typically is, but organizations that invest in this stage will be one step closer to presenting a budget that is fair and reasonable and a step closer to winning the grant!

Stage 2: Develop the Budget

Now that understanding the budget requirements for the grant proposal is in hand and budget information is organized, it is time to actually develop the budget. The initial action here is to select spreadsheet software, such as Microsoft Excel, to document the budget items. The next step is to fill in the budget using the information gathered from Stage 1. It is more likely than not that the funder will provide an online proposal budget spreadsheet, so the more organizations are familiar with spreadsheet software, the easier it will be to navigate the online (and paper) budget spreadsheets.

Selecting a Spreadsheet Software Tool

A number of electronic tools are available to document a budget. The tool selected should be based on the complexity of the budget in addition to long-term needs in terms of compatibility with other software tools. While word processing software like Microsoft Word and WordPerfect can assist with documenting the budget, they do not have the same flexibility as spreadsheet software like Microsoft Excel and Lotus, as two examples. Spreadsheet software allows the documenting of the data, the application of formulas to the numbers, and the creation of figures and graphs using the data in the spreadsheet. Finally, for those who are not "numbers" people, spreadsheet software will help in quickly checking for errors in math.

Establish the Budget Period

Every budget has to have a beginning and ending period called the *budget period*. This budget period for a program will be one of these three: (1) the organization's fiscal year, (2) the program year, or (3) the grant period. For instance, the budget period may cover January 1, 2012, through December 31, 2012. This information should be clearly stated on the budget spreadsheet. Also,

---

Key Note

For general operating grant requests, the program year and fiscal year will be the same.

be sure to note whether the budget covers multiple years (based on the grantee request).

Estimate Revenues and Expenses

In Stage 1, all revenues and expenses that should be included in the budget should be identified. At this point, most revenues and expenses will be estimates and should be documented as such. There are instances when actual revenue and expense amounts are known and, if so, those should be included as actuals.

Revenue is income identified and/or already committed for the program such as memberships, fee-for-service, other grants, and other fundraising endeavors such as special events and individual giving. Depending on the program, your budget may contain several different revenue streams. A list of potential revenue sources includes other foundation support, government funding, and individual funds. In addition, items like in-kind donations of supplies, services, and human capital and other volunteer services should also be listed as revenue sources.

The revenue sources included in the budget will be based on the program and should be estimated according to the expected or known revenue stream. For instance, if the revenue is based on memberships or fee-for-service, the amount can be calculated as follows:

Revenue = quantity of the memberships/fee-for-service × price of membership/fee-for-service or

Revenue = Amount assessed for membership fees and/or services rendered

Example: Revenue Budget Table for Swim 4 Life	
Revenues	**Projected**
Individual Fundraising	$60,000
Corporate Funding	$45,000
Some City School Program Funding	$45,000
YWCA	$45,000
In-Kind Goods	$60,000
In-Kind Services	$55,000
Interest	$800
Total	$310,800

Expenses are the costs of those items required to sustain the program. They are a critical piece of the budget because they identify the costs necessary to manage and sustain a program. Expenses can be recorded in two categories—direct and indirect costs.

Direct Costs

According to the Nonprofit and Philanthropy Good Practice guide from the Johnson Center at Grand Valley State University, direct cost: "Includes all items that can be categorically identified and charged to the specific project, such as personnel, fringe benefits, consultants, subcontractors, travel, equipment, supplies and materials, communications, computer time, and publication charges."

They are typically itemized and can be traced directly to the project they support. In Stage 1, we discussed researching, developing, and collecting revenue and expense estimates. This section further highlights why this stage is necessary.

Since these costs are directly related to the project, they should be easy to identify. Here is a short list of potential expenses that may be listed as direct costs or expenses:

- Staff and travel

- Supplies and materials

- Equipment

Calculating direct costs should be kept fairly simple, especially if developing program budgets is a new experience for the organization. For instance, Swim 4 Life employs nine people: one director, one program assistant, and seven part-time staff. For simplicity, all of the employees are salaried. After salaries are researched in the market for the different roles, documentation may look like the following table:

Example: Estimated Salary Table for Swim 4 Life			
Role	**# of Staff**	**Monthly Wages**	**Yearly Total***
Executive Director	1	$4,500	$40,000
Program Assistant	1	$3,125	$25,000
Half-time staff	7	$2,208 (cumulative)	$26,500
Total			**$91,500**

*Yearly total calculation = # Staff × Monthly Wages × 12 Months. Salary information should be collected from some market research database.

The "Total" amount listed in the table is the number that will be included in the Salary row of the budget spreadsheet.

In general, this is the process that should be followed when estimating *all* direct costs associated with a program. While the actual background

Helpful Hint

In some instances, *personnel costs are split* between programs because staff may spend only a portion of their time on a particular project. If this is the case, the personnel costs should be determined by using the percentage of time spent on the program budget in question.

Key Note

Many established nonprofits already have an indirect rate that can be applied to the budget.

research is not demonstrated in this example, the information in the table was derived from a reference data source. Again, this process can be time consuming, but it is necessary.

Indirect Costs

Indirect costs—also known as *overhead* costs—are costs that are shared within an organization or with another program or project. Using the same reference tool from the Johnson Center, indirect costs are:

"Costs that have been incurred for common or joint objectives of a university or nonprofit organization and the sponsored program, and which, therefore, cannot be identified specifically in reference to a particular project, such as building operations and maintenance, laboratory space, library service, utilities, and administrative services." Here is a short list of potential indirect costs or expenses that may be listed as direct costs.

Indirect costs may include

- Utilities
- Information technology support
- Audit or legal staff
- Rent
- Administrative support
- Equipment rental

This estimate is usually determined by using an indirect cost rate.

Helpful Hint

Let's assume the organization's indirect cost rate equals 20 percent. Since this rate was already established within the organization, Swim 4 Life's indirect costs can be calculated. So if Swim 4 Life's direct costs total $200,000, the indirect cost amount that will be included in the budget is $200,000 × 20 percent or $40,000.

Key Note

Keep in mind that the indirect cost rate calculation is only useful when there are some expenses that are shared among programs or projects and the organization is trying to determine only those programs' indirect costs.

In-Kind Support/Donated Goods and Services

Many organizations operate programs using a combination of paid employees and purchased goods and services, and volunteers and donated goods and services. The volunteer time and donated goods and services are considered support and are a vital part of the budget process and should be included as both revenues *and* expenses where applicable. The following (short) list of items can be considered when including in-kind contributions:

- Volunteer or staff time of those unaffiliated with the program and therefore not included in the staff budget line

- General volunteers

- Donated services, including food, printing, marketing, accounting, and other services

- Donated items including office equipment, vehicles, and other tangible items used for the program

- Donation of office or facility space (rent, utilities, and renovations)

There are a number of factors that should be considered when estimating the costs of these items. For instance, volunteer and staff time estimates can be calculated using the average amount an organization would pay someone providing the same or like service multiplied by the number of hours performing the service, as shown in the formula below:

Volunteer/staff time estimate = $ of service if purchased (in the marketplace) × number of hours volunteered

On the other hand, new product and service costs should be calculated based on the "market value" of that new product or service. Used products should be estimated based on the depreciated or resale value of the item. The depreciated value is the value of an item once you remove the accumulated depreciation.

In-kind contributions should not be ignored or taken lightly during the budget process. There are a number of benefits to including these items in your budget, including

- Reduces the overall cash outlay for program expenses

- Expands resource capacity to sustain an organization's program

- Opens the door for community partners to learn and support the organization's program or cause

- Demonstrates to the funder the value of the donor and volunteer contributions

As mentioned earlier, in-kind contributions are typically shown as revenues and expenses to create a net-zero effect. For example, if a volunteer contributes $2,000 worth of her time, that amount should be shown as $2,000 in volunteer support revenue and $2,000 in volunteer support expenses.

It is important that in-kind contributions are net-zero when balancing the budget because there should not be non-cash income covering cash expenses.

There are a number of resources available to assist with developing an organization's budget. However, do be mindful of the type of organization in which funding is being sought. For instance, when seeking funding from the Federal Government, CIRCULAR NO. A-122 is the reference most used to establish principles for determining costs of grants, contracts, and other agreements with nonprofits. Private funding sources use myriad sources, and it is up to the grantseeker to read and understand the grant guidelines issued by individual funders.

Record Budget Information

Once the budget categories have been identified and researched and revenues and expenses finalized, it is time to record this information. The information should be listed in an easy to follow format, preferably using a spreadsheet tool selected early in the process.

Be sure to follow the grant application guidelines with regard to the format in which this information should be recorded. Not following instructions is the surest way for a proposal to be declined.

Stage 3: Review, Update, and Review Budget Again

This stage in the budget development process is a fairly commonsense yet an often missed step—review the budget for formula and number errors and logic. Essentially, grantseekers should take the time to review the budget from the perspective of the funder. Revenue and expense items that appear out of line with the overall budget should be identified and resolved. Grantseekers should also look for budget items that are "questionable" or outside of what is customary for similar programs. Once the final review has occurred, a clear and concise explanation of the items in the budget should be provided in the budget justification.

Stage 4: Develop the Budget Justification

Now that the budget spreadsheet is complete and the numbers reviewed and verified, a budget justification should be developed to explain how the numbers were derived.

The Budget Justification

After the budget is developed, a detailed narrative of the significant items in the budget—called a budget justification—should be written. In its simplest form, this document provides a narrative explanation of the revenues and expenses that require greater explanation of how expenses and revenues were derived and why they are needed. It also shows that there was sufficient thought put into why the grantee believes the revenues and expenses are what is noted in the budget and explain any significant variances. Here is an example of what Swim 4 Life's budget justification may look like:

Sample Budget Justification

The total budget required to support Swim 4 Life's initiative listed in the grant proposal is $460,800. Additional details of the budget are described below:

EXPECTED SOURCES OF FUNDING

Swim 4 Life has outlined several funding sources that will ensure the sustainability of the services it provides to the community. The following is a list of committed funding for the year:

YWCA	$45,000
Corporate Sponsorship	$45,000
Some City School Program	$45,000
Individuals	$60,000
Total	$195,000

In addition to the above we have in-kind goods and services revenue of $115,000 and interest of $800. We are looking to a number of private sector funders to provide an additional $150,000 needed to run an effective program in the service community.

EXECUTIVE DIRECTOR SALARY—$40,000

The executive director is essential to the success of Swim 4 Life, thus requiring a salary that takes into consideration the responsibility involved in leading a high visibility program. The amount covers the salary and benefits for one full-time director to manage the program for one year. Responsibilities will include leading the day-to-day operations of the program, managing a full-time program assistant and several volunteers, developing and managing program initiatives and performance, and ensuring that all fiscal responsibilities are met.

Again, the budget justification is typically documented in a narrative format and presented as a supplement to the budget. While it does not have to be a dissertation of explanations, it should be clear and concise and explain those items in the budget that require further clarification.

The Budget: Final Thoughts

Now that the basics for developing the program budget have been described, there are a few points that should always be remembered:

- Read and understand the type of budget the funder is requiring for the grant application.

- Provide a true and honest picture of expected revenues and expenses.

- Justify, in writing, any budget items that standout as unusual or costly.

Remember, the presentation of the budget is just as important as the presentation of the overall program that will be supported by the grant.

Program Budget Dos and Don'ts

The following is a list of Dos and Don'ts when developing the grant application's program budget.

Do . . .
- Understand that a budget is an important part of the grant application process

- Read the grant application for budget requirements, including formats and specific instructions

- Identify elements to include in the budget based on the program's needs

- Collect and record data to substantiate revenues and expenses listed in the budget

- Provide a budget justification to explain any major funding variances or requests

- Itemize revenues and expenses

Don't . . .
- Overlook the importance of developing a logical and reasonable budget based on the funder's instructions

- Include items that are not specifically requested in the grant application
- Lump all revenues and expenses together; rather, itemize for clarity
- Forget to review and check the final document before submitting

Use Worksheet 8.1 to prepare a budget for the program. On the companion website, grantseekers will find two sample Excel template with the formulas already entered as tools for practice. One template is for a one-year budget; the second is for a three-year budget. There is also a sample Excel budget for the Swim 4 Life program on the website. For best results, grantseekers should start by creating a budget using Worksheet 8.1, followed by experimenting with the online spreadsheet. Simply enter projected revenues and expenses and add categories if necessary and appropriate. Asking the Budget Review Questions at the end of this step will highlight those areas in the budget that need further attention.

WORKSHEET 8.1:
Revenue and Expense Budget

On the Web

	Cash Required	In-Kind Contributions	Total Budget
REVENUE			
Foundations			
Government			
Corporations			
Individual contributions			
Donated printing and supplies			
Volunteer services			
Other (specify):			
Total revenue			
EXPENSES			
Salaries (prorated if less than full-time)			
_____			
_____			
_____			
_____			
Payroll taxes and benefits (percentage of salaries)			
Bookkeeping contractor			
Other (specify):			
Total personnel			
Office rent (percentage for program)			
Supplies			
Printing			
Utilities			
Telephone			
Copy services			
Postage			
Travel			
Membership dues			
Other (specify):			
Total nonpersonnel			
Total expenses			

Budget Review Questions

1. Is the budget consistent with the proposal's program plan (methods)?

2. Is there a budget narrative that explains items that may not be immediately clear?

3. Does the budget include in-kind revenues and expenses?

4. Does the budget address the question of how overhead costs will be recovered?

5. Is the budget realistic? In other words, can the organization accomplish the intended objectives with the proposed budget?

6. Has the organization kept the budget worksheet, so that it has a record of how costs were determined for the expense items?

Now it's time to focus on the organization background statement, which is Step Nine.

References

National Institute of Health, http://grants.nih.gov/grants/glossary.htm

Burke Smith, N., and Tremore, J. 2008. *Everything Grant Writing Book* (2nd ed.). Avon, MA: Adams Media.

Greater Washington Society of CPAs, http://www.nonprofitaccountingbasics .org/reporting-operations/budgeting-terms-concepts

Step 9
Writing the Organization Background Component

IN ADDITION TO THE PLANNING SECTIONS of the proposal, grantseekers need to develop an organization background component. This step provides an overview of the purpose of an organization background statement and of what it should contain to best establish a nonprofit's credibility. Using examples and a worksheet, grantseekers will learn how to present their organization's strengths to funders.

Purpose of the Organization Background Statement

What are the mission, values, and other distinguishing characteristics of the organization? And what is it about this particular organization that enables it to successfully execute on what it promises to deliver? The organization background component answers these two questions and more. This is the section of the proposal that highlights all the positive qualities of the organization, which means this section can get rather lengthy if restraint is not employed. Try to limit this component to no more than three pages. A good organization background statement describes the nonprofit well enough to assure prospective funders that this nonprofit can successfully undertake the proposed program.

Funders may refer to this section as the "Introduction" or the "Applicant Description," but the same basic information is expected regardless of its name. This section of the proposal should allow the reviewer to get a strong impression that the organization

- Meets an unmet need or fills an essential role in the community

- Is fiscally secure

- Is well managed

- Provides important community services
- Understands the community it serves
- Reflects that community in its board and staff
- Has the respect of the community

Content of the Organization Background Component

Organizations should include the following:

- A description of the organization and its mission and vision, and how it came to be—its history.

- The demographics of the community served by the organization, followed by the ways in which both the board members and the staff reflect those demographics. This information is growing steadily in importance to funders, as they want to ensure that the nonprofit is in the best position to truly understand and connect with the community it seeks to serve.

- A description of the organization's position and role in the community. Who are the organization's collaborating partners in the community?

- A discussion of the ways the organization is unique in comparison to others providing similar services.

- Descriptions of innovative programs or special services the organization has provided. Has it received any awards or special recognition?

- A very *brief* history of funding by other sources.

The primary goal in crafting this section of the proposal is to establish credibility with potential funders. Organizations need to use sound judgment as to what is appropriate given the specific proposal—and the funder. The guiding question should be, "What is the key information that this funder needs about the organization and its qualifications to solidify the case for support?" Similarly, when requesting funding for a highly technical project that makes use of new ways to engage clients via the Internet, information about the organization's past experience in web-based communications, as well as the qualifications of specific staff members who would be responsible for the project, would be critical to reinforcing the nonprofit's capacity to undertake the proposed project successfully. If proposing a collaborative project, thought should be given to using examples of other collaborative projects in which the organization participated as well as the successful outcomes derived from those collaborations.

Testimonials and statistics relating to the work of the nonprofit may be incorporated, although they should be kept at a minimum. The organization background component should be primarily an informative and interesting narrative describing the qualifications of the organization. Understand that the funder would probably prefer a summary of the highlights in the nonprofit's history that relate to the project needing funding. In this instance, don't be afraid to use bullet points to highlight items in what would otherwise become very dense narrative.

Don't eat up valuable proposal space with information on the organization's structure or specific details about board members and staff unless such detail is requested. Supporting documents, such as an organization chart and résumés of key staff, can provide this information and add credibility to the proposal, and it should be provided in the proposal's appendixes (see Step Eleven). However, some funders specify what appendixes they will, and will not, accept—so incorporating this information into the background statement might be warranted. Should this be the case, keep it brief. Summarize how many staff and board members the organization has and also the number of active volunteers engaged with it.

If the organization is too new to have any accomplishments, try focusing on the qualifications of the staff and board to provide some sense of credibility for the start-up endeavor. As a start-up, it will be critical to clearly state the unmet needs or unique problem the organization is being created to meet.

Tips for Writing the Organization Background Component
Background Statement

Start with when and why the organization was founded. Its mission statement should be front and center in the first or second paragraph. From there, move away from the philosophy of the organization and begin explaining what it does.

This is one of the few sections of a proposal that can be created as a standard component and used repeatedly. Grantseekers will be required to make small edits to tailor the background statement for specific funders on occasion or to highlight items of special interest to a particular funder. Otherwise, this section is fairly standard for most proposals.

Read the following Sample Organization Background Component. Then, using Worksheet 9.1, gather the information for this section of your organization's proposal. Next, write the narrative, using the Sample Organization Background Component as a guide. Finally, review the work using the Organization Background Review Questions. Organizations should be able to answer "yes" to each question.

Sample Organization Background Component

Swim 4 Life was established as a 501(c)3 organization in 2008 by 2000 Olympic swimming hopeful Jane Swimmer, who emerged as one of the brightest female swim stars in the United States at the 2000 Games. The mission of Swim 4 Life is to empower youth in underserved communities, through high-quality programs, to utilize the discipline of swimming to improve physical fitness, nurture self-esteem, and acquire the confidence to advance their lives.

Jane was an eleven-time U.S. National Champion and two-time USA Swimmer of the Year. In 2005, she started for-profit swim schools at various community centers in two other counties in Any State. Inspired by the results achieved at her for-profit schools, Ms. Swimmer began to explore the idea of bringing a high-quality program to youth in underserved communities that would offer the same standard of excellence found in the best private club programs, such as her own. However, she continued to focus on the for-profit schools until January 2007, when she conducted a pilot water safety program at the West Hanover Swim School with fifty middle and high school students who were bussed in from ABC Youth (ABCY), a nonprofit organization that provides enrichment programs in the Gathentown School District. The results clearly demonstrated that the program could be replicated effectively in a nonprofit setting.

Because the school lacked the capacity to accommodate growth of Swim 4 Life programs, and considering the cost of recruiting and transporting youth across the city to the selected site, it was determined that the optimal pools to use for program sites would be those located in the communities where the target population lived. The first site chosen was Arthur Schomburg Middle School in South Spring, where a pool that had been out of service for fifteen years was about to re-open. In 2008, a second site was added at the Rockmore Education Complex, a high school near downtown Abbington. The Adapted Learn-to-Swim program began at the high school in summer 2008 to meet the needs of students with disabilities.

As of 2006, the Gathentown Unified School District must comply with a statewide mandate to include aquatics programs in all high school physical education curricula for 9th and 10th grade students. However, because of poor staff training and long-term cutbacks in funding for physical education, the district was ill-prepared to teach students to swim despite its large investment in building nine new high schools with competition-size pools.

Too often, youth in the communities our program targets lack the opportunities, guidance, and/ or family support equal to that of their surrounding counties to provide them the foundation to help guide them in the right direction. By providing these kids with valuable access to swimming via the Swim 4 Life program, we endeavor to empower these kids to learn the values of self-discipline, decision making, hard work, and dedication that have a real chance of forever changing their lives. The aim is to inspire children to explore their potential through swimming and give all children the same opportunity to enjoy the sport.

The organization uses swimming to reach out to children who are at risk of failure in school, gang affiliation, unhealthy lifestyles, including childhood obesity, and other physically, mentally, and emotionally unhealthy outcomes. More than 450 youth have participated in its short history, and 85 percent of those in the non-adapted classes have passed a water safety survival test. Programs are delivered by two full-time and seven part-time employees, with a seven-member board of directors providing oversight and governance.

WORKSHEET 9.1:
Organization Background Exercise

[Organization Name]	Accomplishments	Personnel
Location		
Legal status		
Date of founding		
Mission		
Target population		
Programs		
Partnerships		
How unique		
Special recognition		
Summary of need statement		
Financial		
Board and staff		

Organization Background Review Questions

1. Does the organization background section give the nonprofit credibility by stating its history, specific qualifications, purpose, programs, target population, total number of people served, and major accomplishments?

2. Does the background suggest sources of community support for the proposed program?

3. Does this section highlight any awards received? This can include winning government funding through a competitive process.

Now it's time to pull the entire proposal together with the proposal summary, which is Step Ten.

Step 10
Writing the Proposal Summary

THE PROPOSAL IS NOW NEARLY COMPLETE. The proposal summary does what its title suggests—it summarizes the entire proposal. In this step grantseekers learn the basics of constructing a solid and compelling summary. Using a worksheet and following examples, grantseekers also write a summary for their own proposals.

Purpose and Content of the Summary

A proposal summary (also referred to as an executive summary) is a clear, one- or two-page abstract of the full proposal. Its purpose is to encapsulate the strongest key elements of the grantseeker's proposal, which will then lead the funder to engage in reading the full proposal.

All proposals of more than five pages in length should contain a summary, and in most cases funders require a summary as a part of the proposal. Positioned as the opening element of the proposal, it is typically the section written last to ensure that all critical proposal elements are incorporated. A proposal summary should contain the following elements:

- Identification of the applicant (the organization)
- The specific purpose of the grant
- The applicant's qualifications to carry out this purpose (the program)
- The anticipated end result
- The total program or project budget and how much the applicant is requesting from the grantmaker to be used toward that amount

Grantseekers should endeavor to include each of the elements outlined in the previous section in short paragraphs.

A crisp and well-articulated summary assists the funder in understanding the need for the program, its goals, and objectives. A good proposal summary paints a picture of the full proposal and successfully entices the funder to read more. Grantseekers should always keep in mind that funders receive dozens—and in many cases hundreds—of grant proposals to review during any given funding cycle.

There are many different approaches to employ when writing the proposal summary. Some will start with the compelling problem the program is designed to address, whereas others will start by introducing the organization, highlighting its reputation and standing, and presenting its overall qualifications. When in doubt, consider following the same order used in the proposal.

If writing the proposal summary is a struggle, know that even the most seasoned grantwriters sometimes struggle with this section because it demands brevity. It requires the writer to capture the most essential elements of each component of the proposal, in a condensed style—yet in a way that will capture the reader's attention and distinguish this proposal from the rest.

Tips for Writing the Summary

- Decide what the key points are in each section of the proposal's components. Include only those key points in the summary.

- Stress the key points important to the funder. Make sure the summary highlights the potential funder's priorities.

Study the following Sample Summary for the Swim 4 Life. Then complete Worksheet 10.1 to pull together the material for the summary. Finally, review the work by asking the Summary Review Questions. Grantseekers should be able to answer yes to each question.

Sample Summary

Swim 4 Life was established as a 501(c) nonprofit organization in 2008 by 2000 Olympic swimming hopeful Jane Swimmer, who emerged as one of the brightest female swim stars in the United States at the 2000 Games. The mission of the Swim 4 Life program is to empower youth in the underserved communities throughout King County, through high-quality programs, to utilize the discipline of swimming to improve physical fitness, nurture self-esteem, and acquire the confidence to advance their lives. This mission is fulfilled through programs currently operated at Arthur Schomburg Middle School in South Spring and the Rockmore Education Complex high school near downtown Abbington. More than 450 youth have participated since operations began in 2007.

The overall goal of the program is to empower children in disadvantaged neighborhoods through swimming with the confidence and baseline skills to save their lives, improve their academic performance, and increase the potential for an improved quality of life. One of the program's primary objectives to achieve the goal is to teach a minimum of 150 children to swim every year so that they have the opportunity to enjoy the sport and be "water-safe," thus gaining a much needed confidence boost. More than 450 youth have participated in the program's short history, and 85 percent of those children passed a water safety survival test. Programs are delivered by two full-time and seven part-time employees, with a seven-member board of directors providing oversight and governance.

The Rockmore Education Complex is located in the city of Abbington, the most densely populated city in the state, with 8,552 people occupying every square mile, compared with a state average of 2,093 people per square mile. It has the highest crime rate in the state, and the poverty rate is 46 percent, nearly twice that of all other cities in the state, with the exception of South Spring, which has a 31 percent crime rate. Fifty-one percent of children under the age of eighteen live in poverty, compared with 31 percent in the rest of the city. Young people in this community clearly live under stressful conditions and could benefit greatly from structured and supervised physical activity, as well as safe opportunities for fun and positive engagement.

The Swim 4 Life program currently operates programs at one middle school (Schomberg); in Fall 2008 it began regular programs at one high school (RLC), while a third program started at both sites in the Fall of 2009. The goal of the program is to expand to one additional school in 2012: Cooperville Middle School, which is also located in Abbington. Our program at one school even provides swim instruction specifically for students with disabilities. Through our partnership with the Gathenton School District, we are offered the opportunity to replicate the programs throughout the cities of Rockmore and South Spring in King County, contributing to improved health and fitness of thousands of youth who have been excluded from learning the sport of swimming because of limited access to safe pools.

The entire Swim 4 Life Program budget is $468,800, of which $150,000 remains to be raised. Your gift of $25,000 will go a long way toward helping us meet our objective of program expansion, thus serving 25 percent more kids. Thank you for your consideration of our request.

WORKSHEET 10.1:
Summary Questionnaire

1. What is the identity of the organization, and what is its mission?

2. What is the proposed program or project (title, purpose, target population)?

3. Why is the proposed program or project important?

4. What will be accomplished by this program or project during the time period of the grant?

5. Why should the organization do the program or project (credibility statement)?

6. How much will the program or project cost during the grant time period? How much is being requested from this funder?

Summary Review Questions

1. Does the summary clearly identify the applicant(s)?

2. Does it describe the specific need to be addressed and the specific objectives to be achieved?

3. Does it mention the total program or project cost and the amount of funding requested?

Helpful Hint

Be consistent. Now is not the time to introduce new information. Everything in this section should already be part of the full proposal.

---

4. Is it brief (no more than two pages maximum)?

5. Does it thank the funder for considering the applicant's request for funding?

It is now time to assemble the entire proposal package, which is Step Eleven.

Step 11
Putting the Package Together

IN THIS STEP GRANTSEEKERS LEARN the importance of presenting their proposal with a clear but brief cover letter, in addition to the attachments that funders may require for inclusion. This step takes on a particular significance in light of the seismic shift in the funding world from paper grant submissions to online submissions via email and online portals for grant submissions.

Purpose and Content of the Cover Letter

First, it should be clarified that in this time of grantseeking, a cover letter is more likely to take the form of an email because, as is being referenced in several places throughout this workbook, many proposals are likely to be submitted electronically. Organizations need to craft a brief, yet informative cover letter that will serve as the first piece of information the funder reads. This letter should accomplish the following:

- Briefly introduce the organization making the request.
- Highlight the support of the board of directors for the project.
- Specifically mention the financial request—how much and for what.

Make it the goal to keep the cover letter to a two or three paragraph maximum length. Keep the details in the proposal and don't take up time with an unnecessarily lengthy cover letter. Start the letter with a very brief introduction of the organization and inform the funder of the amount and purpose of the request. Use the next paragraph to very briefly highlight the proposal and any salient points. The closing paragraph should thank the funder for consideration of the request and should also clearly indicate who to contact within the organization should the funder have questions. This should be the same person the funder will contact with responses. Typically, the person who signs the cover letter—which should be the organization's executive director, board president, or both—is not the contact person who follows up on the request. Therefore, it is vital to clearly indicate the contact person by name and title, as well as provide that individual's direct email address and phone extension. Grantseekers should take care to minimize confusion by making it as simple as possible for funders to reach the right person in the organization.

This final paragraph should also be used to invite a meeting, phone call, or site visit.

Use the following Sample Cover Letter as an example.

Sample Cover Letter

Wendy Wonder
President
XYZ Foundation
0000 Nocounty Avenue, Suite 2330
Anytown, Any State 02009

Dear Ms. Wonder:

On behalf of the board of directors and staff, I am honored to submit the following proposal requesting consideration of a grant for $25,000 to Swim 4 Life to assist us in expanding from two to three program sites in the Gathenton School District in King County, Any State. This program is an innovative swimming instruction program established by Jane Swimmer, a former U.S. Olympic swimming hopeful and hometown hero.

Established in 2008, the mission of the Swim 4 Life program is to empower youth in the underserved communities throughout King County, through high-quality programs, to utilize the discipline of swimming to improve physical fitness, nurture self-esteem, and acquire the confidence to advance their lives. More than 450 youth have participated since operations began.

Because of your commitment to encouraging young people to reach their fullest potential, we sincerely hope that the XYZ Foundation will join us as our partner in this important program. Should you have any questions, please feel free to call me at (111) 111–1111. We deeply appreciate your consideration of our request and look forward to hearing from you in September if not before.

Sincerely,
Shawn Jones, Executive Director

Purpose and Content of the Appendixes

Appendixes, or attachments, are a necessary and important addition to any grant proposal. These are documents that are not components of the proposal per se, yet they provide valuable information that the funder will need when considering a request. Most funders, regardless of size, and certainly nearly all public funders (local, state, and federal government grants), supply a list of required appendixes. When no list is provided, consider including the following documents:

- The organization's IRS 501(c)(3) tax-exempt status determination letter or fiscal agent's letter, if there is a sponsor, to establish nonprofit status

- The organization's most recent audited financial statement

- A list of the organization's board members, their work and school affiliations, and any other applicable information

- The organization's overall budget for the current fiscal year

- The organization's latest annual report (if it prepares an annual report)

- A list of all other funders who have received or are receiving proposals for the program, the amounts of these requests, and the current status of each request

In addition to these items, a funder might request profiles of the key staff members assigned to implement or oversee the proposed project or a list of current funders or both. Some funders may also require an attachment section for a letter proposal. Many of the items in the previous list are generally included with these shorter proposals. Letters of intent, however, will probably require a much reduced appendixes section that includes only the IRS determination letter and possibly a list of members of the board of directors and the organization's budget.

Packaging the Proposal

A simple, clutter-free, and neatly packaged proposal creates the perception of a well-organized, successful organization. This holds true for an email proposal submission. When submitting via email, grantseekers should always convert the proposal and attachments to PDF format. PDF stands for portable document format, and it not only makes documents present more professionally, but it also prevents the documents from being edited in any way and it locks formatting in place. As a general rule, organizations should never submit documents electronically that are not in PDF format.

Review all appendixes to ensure that

- They are nicely copied on fresh paper or that each computer file is in PDF format.

- The pages are numbered and appropriately identified.

- The proposal is nicely formatted, with no typos (don't rely on spell-check but run it anyway).

- The name of the foundation, staff person, and address information are correct (and don't hand address the envelope or label). In the case of an electronic document, verify that the appropriate formatting remains in place.

- The cover letter is printed on organization's letterhead. For an electronic proposal submission, a cover letter will probably not be an option. If an organization is submitting a proposal via email, the email copy should be succinct.

- If the submission is via email, make sure all documents are properly labeled and that the appropriate recipient is known and the email address is correct.

Grantseekers should consider creating a table of contents and numbered appendixes for the proposal. This should be done for both an electronic and paper proposal submission.

Specific to Paper Proposal Submissions

If the funder is requesting a paper submission, carefully read the funder's guidelines to confirm the number of proposal copies that should be submitted. Funders might request an original and several copies of a full proposal, so make sure to follow their instructions. If more than one copy of the proposal is requested, clearly mark which proposal is the original. Organizations should also be prepared for requests to submit proposals on a thumb drive.

In an effort to cut down on use of paper products in general, proposals (other than letter proposals with only a few appendixes) should be neatly arranged and held together with a large binder clip, rather than a folder. Start with the full proposal, the budget, and then the appendixes in the order listed in the guidelines. Leave the cover letter outside the binder clip for the original proposal only. Each copy of the proposal can be fully binder-clipped, with the cover letter copy inside the clip. Grantseekers can paperclip each section of the proposal if desired (narrative proposal, budget, appendixes), as that might make accessing the proposal overall easier for the funder.

Placing a proposal in a three-ring notebook, having it spiral-bound, or spending unnecessary money to have it color copied does not add value. Presentation is important, but only from a neatness and orderliness standpoint.

Specific to Electronic Submissions

Electronic submissions can sometimes have technological challenges. For that reason, take care to submit electronic proposals sooner rather than closer to the deadline date. *Always keep in mind that technology is known to pick the most inopportune moments to fail.* If the funder has a portal, be sure to double-check whether it is one that will allow applicants to save submissions in progress, or whether the full submission must be completed in one sitting. This distinction is critical, as one allows grantseekers to edit as they go, save their work, and come back to complete the submission. The other does not allow this functionality and will require a dedicated amount of time and attention to detail.

Use the checklist in Worksheet 11.1 to make sure the proposal is complete and ready to mail.

WORKSHEET 11.1:
Final Proposal Checklist

On the Web

Place a checkmark next to each step after it is completed.

_____ Determine which program or project ideas have the best chance of being funded.

_____ Form a planning team that includes clients affected by the program or project, community leaders, key staff and volunteers, and other organizations with similar or complementary projects.

_____ Design a program or project plan.

_____ Conduct thorough research to determine funding sources most likely to be interested in the program or project. Note funder deadlines.

_____ Visit the website of each prospective funder to review its grant guidelines, annual report, grantee list, and so forth. If a funder has no website, email or call to request information helpful in preparing the proposal (annual report, grant guidelines, and so on).

_____ Read all other grantmaker materials (Form 990, media coverage, and so on) to ensure that the proposal falls within the funder's interest areas as demonstrated by previous grants made.

_____ Prepare the proposal core components by stating the need or problem to be addressed, the objectives and the methods for meeting the need, the ways the project will be evaluated and funded in the future, and the budget.

_____ Determine the features of the program or project that may set it apart from other projects and will appeal to the funder.

_____ Make sure those features are highlighted for the funder.

_____ Prepare the final proposal components: the introduction, summary, and cover letter.

_____ Ensure the proposal is clear and well written by having at least one person review it and provide feedback.

_____ Include all appendixes requested by the funder.

_____ Review grant guidelines and confirm the number of proposal copies to be submitted and any specific formatting requests in order to meet the requirements.

_____ Give copies of the proposal to members of the planning team and other individuals or groups who should be aware of the program or project.

_____ Email or call the funder within two weeks after mailing the proposal.

Reality Check

It is essential to follow the funder's guidelines for packaging a proposal, just as with all other parts of the application process. Nearly all funders—foundations, corporations, and government—will stipulate that they do not want staples in proposals. In many cases funders are tasked with making multiple copies for others to review; staples make their jobs much harder. Whatever requirements funders have specified in their grant guidelines is exactly what should be submitted. Do not given the funder any reasons to disqualify the proposal.

Sending the Proposal

For a proposal to be successful it must reflect the work of a fully developed and articulated program plan, which is 70 percent of the up-front work and is sometimes easily overlooked. Only then is the proposal written (the other 30 percent), clearly and concisely, for a targeted funder who has been thoroughly researched and vetted and with whom a relationship has been established.

Please pay particular attention to the Resources for Grantseekers in Resource C in this workbook and on the *Winning Grants Step by Step, Fourth Edition* website to find out more about how to research funders and learn about various preferences and values. When the organization's proposal is packaged and mailed to prospective funders, go through Step Twelve (the next step in this workbook) to review some suggested strategies for maintaining contact with those funders and moving the proposal through their grantmaking process.

Step 12
Sustaining Relationships with Funders

NOW IS THE PERFECT TIME to take inventory: a compelling program plan addressing a pressing community problem was created. From there, a solid grant proposal using the steps as outlined in this workbook was crafted. Then said proposal was submitted as directed in the funder's grant guidelines. Mission accomplished? Well, not quite yet.

Following Up on the Proposal

In many cases, funders will provide a timeline for their grantmaking process. Imbedded within this timeline will be language outlining that the funder requires a certain number of weeks or months to review all proposals. There may even be a request that organizations not call during that specific period—a request that should be honored. In addition, more funders are incorporating site visits into the grantmaking process, and they want to save all discussion and questions for that time. For funders with online grant proposal submission processes—either via email or via a specialized portal—grantseekers are likely to receive an e-notification of some sort that will confirm receipt. However, if submitting by mail, it is recommended that organizations take the time to make a follow-up call to confirm receipt.

Managing a Site Visit

A site visit is exactly what its name implies: the funder comes to the organization's site (or the site of the proposed program) to visit with leaders, staff, board members, and those the organization serves. Not every organization requesting funding gets a site visit, as it is primarily a part of the vetting process for proposals that are in the advanced stage of consideration. Grantseekers should also understand that a site visit is by no means an assurance of program funding. What it does mean is that there is enough of a match between the grantmaker, the organization, and the proposed program that the funder believes it warrants further investigation.

When a site visit is requested, the key staff assigned to the program are essential to the process because they (ideally) were the people who created the program plan, and they are the ones (again, ideally) who will be responsible for the hands-on implementation of the project. They should be present during the visit, as should the executive director and the person who can answer financial or budgetary questions. If the program targets a specific group of people, representation in the form of one or more individuals from the population to be served or engaged is always welcome, as they can provide the most useful testimony for the program, its significance, and its power for change.

If a nonprofit is selected for a site visit, use the following to-do list to prepare:

- Confirm the participation of all key persons involved with the program.
- Send the full proposal to everyone participating, and request that they (re)familiarize themselves with it.
- If the funder has provided questions in advance of the site visit, share those as well.
- Meet with everyone in advance of the actual site visit to ensure that everyone is on the same page in terms of knowledge about the program and its goals, objectives, and methods and that everyone understands who will be answering which questions and moderating the visit.
- Make sure beverages are available for the visit, but keep it basic: no need for catering or any other special event details.

If the funder requests a tour of some sort, decide what the important elements are for the funder's representatives to see and plan the tour in advance—again informing everyone who will be a part of it what is happening and when. Make sure everything is in order and try to schedule the tour for a time when they can see the programs in action; check with staff to make sure it won't be disruptive to have visitors or violate clients' confidentiality or privacy in any way.

Keeping the Funder Informed

Keeping prospective funders up to date on which of these other grantmakers is funding the program or has declined a request at this time is always recommended. As new grant requests are submitted, it is in the best interest of the organization to notify all foundations that are currently considering funding for the program. Refer back to each individual funder's guidelines to be sure of each funder's requests regarding being open to phone calls and email communication during the review process.

Responding to the Funder's Decision

It is inevitable: funding decisions will be made. When decisions are received, organization staff will be either sighing for relief or sighing for temporary defeat. In either case, grantseekers need to move forward with their relationship building.

When the Proposal Is Funded

There is nothing like getting that call, letter, or email announcing that the grant is being awarded. It is a wonderful feeling of accomplishment, regardless of the size of the grant. An email to the funder is certainly in order as soon as word is received regarding the request being approved. As busy as funders are, they all want to hear about how the programs—and organizations—they've funded are progressing. In most foundations with paid staff, the grantmaking process requires staff to advocate for the programs they recommend for funding. Make no mistake: staff at funding institutions advocate on behalf of the organizations being recommended for grants, so consider them partners and keep them apprised on a quarterly basis (minimum) with a brief note, an email, a call, a personalized newsletter, or whatever form of communication is most effective and appropriate.

Following an email to the funder, which should happen within the same day as notification, a formal letter of thanks should also be sent to the funder and signed by the executive director.

As a general rule, most funders anticipate some sort of public recognition of its grants. Standard forms of recognition include a feature in the grantee's newsletter and inclusion on a donor list on the recipient's website or in the annual report. Consider the level of recognition in proportion to the amount of funds received; that should guide the selection process for the appropriate recognition level. A large grant may warrant special recognition at an organization's annual event or ceremony of some sort, or a media announcement. Ultimately, if anything beyond a newsletter mention and inclusion in a donor list is being considered, it should be discussed with the funder in advance of making any decisions. Organizations should not make any assumptions about funder recognition, particularly if the grant award letter does not provide specific guidance on the subject.

If the funding institution (or the grant) is to remain anonymous, the funder will clearly stipulate that fact in its grant award letter. Of course in such situations the funder's name should not be mentioned anywhere publicly, and care should be taken in all internal records to mark the grant-maker as anonymous.

When a grant is awarded, the nonprofit will

- Receive initial notification of the award. This is being done increasingly via email, though it may also happen via phone call.

- Receive official confirmation in the form of a grant agreement letter.

- Have the organization's executive director and other appropriate staff (such as the person responsible for program implementation and the person responsible for organization finances) review this document to ensure that the nonprofit will be able to comply with all of its stipulations, as it is a legally binding agreement.

- Return the signed Grant Agreement Letter within three to five days of receipt.

- Provide quarterly, semiyearly, or yearly progress reports. Each funder has different requirements, but these will be spelled out clearly in the Grant Agreement Letter. Timely reports are especially critical if the nonprofit hopes to be eligible to reapply to this funder for further support.

Notify the funder of all major changes or issues identified in the program as soon as possible. Staffing changes, a particular method that is not working, and participant recruitment that is well below what was originally targeted—these are all examples of situations about which your funding partner should be informed.

When the Proposal Is Not Funded

There will be dozens—and in some cases hundreds—of other organizations that receive a letter of declination. So what happened? Why was the organization's program not selected? On average, a typical foundation can make grants in response to approximately 8 to 10 percent of the total requests it receives in every funding cycle. Sometimes the approval rate is even smaller than that, especially for the largest foundations in the United States.

An organization's declination letter is likely to be very general and provide only vague reasons for the denial. So grantseekers might want to follow up with the funder via email to see if any additional feedback can be shared as to why the organization's proposal was not funded. Consider asking the following three questions via email:

- Were there any parts of the funder's guidelines that were missed? (Find out up front if the proposal was disqualified for any reason.)

- Was additional information or further clarity needed in the program plan or grant proposal to make it more competitive?

- Is it recommended that the organization resubmit a proposal for this program at another time? If so, when?

Be sure to thank the funder for considering the request. Let civility be the rule, and remember that there is always the next cycle.

The reality is this: there are many stellar programs that do not get funded. There are compelling grant proposals that do not get funded. The demand for foundation and corporate (and government) grants is simply too high, and competition for these dollars grows more challenging each and every year.

That being said, organizations should be on a mission to be organized, truthful, respectful, consistent, and persistent in their grantseeking endeavors. It is vital to keep in mind that a denial from a funder does not mean a program lacks merit, nor does it mean that a program will never get funded.

There are more reasons than pages in this workbook that might explain why a proposal is not funded; just continue building the funder relationships. Consider keeping all the funders identified as a match for the organization's programs, even if those very funders have denied funding requests in the past, on the organization's mailing list; also invite them to events, and continue to share organization successes with them via periodic updates through emails and other communications.

Final Thoughts

The takeaways from *Winning Grants Step by Step, Fourth Edition*, are twofold. First, the goal is to provide the time-tested, nuts and bolts of proposal development and a framework for how they should come together. Some of the material from the first three editions remains as relevant now as it was then—it works. Second, the goal is to provide some additional context for the grantseeking process itself. As is mentioned in several places in this workbook, a well-written, well-organized grant proposal is a critical component of the funding equation, but there is more to do to ultimately "win" that grant.

Providing organizations with the knowledge that grantseeking is a process that in many cases spans months—and in some cases years—of cultivation and relationship building is an important piece of the funding equation. Finally, what most differentiates this edition from the first three is the undeniable role technology now plays in the "winning grants" process. From prospect research to proposal submission to the actual grant award itself, which may come in the form of a wire transfer directly into the organizations' account rather than a paper check, there is no denying the increasing influence of technology in the grantseeking process.

Bibliography

Adapted from UCLA Center for Health Policy Research. *Health Data, Train the Trainer Project. Performing A Community Assessment Curriculum.* 2004. www.healthpolicy.ucla.edu/healthdata/tw_cba4.pdf

Burke, T., Smith, N., and Tremore, J. 2008. *Everything Grant Writing Book* (2nd ed.). Avon, MA: Adams Media.

Center on Philanthropy at Indiana University. 2012. The Trustees of Indiana University. http://www.philanthropy.iupui.edu

Center on Philanthropy and Public Policy at the University of Southern California. 2013. http://cppp.usc.edu/

Greater Washington Society of CPAs. 2013. http://www.nonprofitaccountingbasics.org/reporting-operations/budgeting-terms-concepts

Heyman, D. R. 2011. *Nonprofit Management 101: A Complete and Practical Guide for Leaders and Professionals.* San Francisco: Jossey-Bass.

Hutton, S., and Phillips, F. 2011. *Nonprofit Kit for Dummies* (2nd ed.). Hoboken, NJ: Wiley.

Meyer, P. J. 2003. "What Would You Do If You Knew You Couldn't Fail? Creating S.M.A.R.T. Goals." *Attitude Is Everything: If You Want to Succeed Above and Beyond.* Meyer Resource Group, Incorporated.

National Institute of Health. 2013. http://grants.nih.gov/grants/glossary.htm

Nonprofit and Philanthropy Good Practice at the Johnson Center and Grand Valley State University. 2011. http://www.npgoodpractice.org/glossary

Organizational Research Services for Annie E. Casey. "Theory of Change: A Practical Tool for Action, Results and Learning." 2004. www.aecf.org/upload/publicationfiles/cc2977k440.pdf

Goetz, R. January 2010. *Defining Project Goals and Objectives.* www.projectsmart.co.uk

The Foundation Center. 2013. http://foundationcenter.org

The Grantsmanship Center. 1972–2010. www.tgci.com

Theory of Change. Theory of Change Community, LLC. 2012. www.theoryofchange.org

Resource A: What Is a Foundation?

THERE ARE ESSENTIALLY two types of foundations: private and public. As defined by Foundation Center (http://foundationcenter.org/getstarted /tutorials/ft_tutorial/what.html), a private foundation

- Is a nongovernmental, nonprofit organization
- Has a principal fund or endowment
- Is managed by its own trustees and directors
- Maintains or aids charitable, educational, religious, or other activities serving the public good
- Makes grants, primarily to other nonprofit organizations
- Is required to file a 990-PF form with the IRS annually

The three private foundation types are (1) independent or family foundations, (2) corporate foundations, and (3) operating foundations.

1. The term *family foundation* does not have any legal meaning, but the Council on Foundations defines a family foundation as one in which "the donor or the donor's relatives play a significant role in governing and/ or managing the foundation." The Foundation Center refers to independent and family foundations as those receiving endowments from individuals or families (and, in the case of family foundations, they continue to show measurable donor or donor-family involvement).

2. A corporate foundation is also referred to as a company-sponsored foundation. A corporate foundation is established by a corporation but tends to operate separately from the company and to have its own dedicated staff. In most cases it is a separate legal entity that maintains close ties to the parent company, and the members of the foundation and company boards sometimes intentionally overlap. These foundations tend to give to a broad spectrum of organizations; however, some establish giving policies that reflect the parent company's interest. Others allow the employees of the

corporation to have decision-making authority over some—if not all—of the foundation's grantmaking. Often, corporate foundations provide grant support in the areas where their corporation has a base of operation.

3. An operating foundation uses its resources to conduct research or provide a direct service. It is not uncommon for this type of foundation to engage in fundraising as a means of generating the revenue it needs to make grants.

A public foundation (also known as a public charity) as defined by the Foundation Center

- Is a nongovernmental, nonprofit organization
- Receives funding from numerous sources and must continue to seek money from diverse sources in order to retain its public charity status
- Is managed by its own trustees and directors
- Operates grants programs benefiting unrelated organizations or individuals as one of its primary purposes
- Makes grants, primarily to other nonprofit organizations
- Is required to file a 990 form with the IRS

Here are three examples of public foundations:

Community Foundation. A community foundation is a tax-exempt, nonprofit, autonomous, publicly supported, nonsectarian philanthropic institution with a long-term goal of building permanent, named component funds, established by many separate donors, for the broad-based charitable benefit of the residents of a defined geographic area, typically no larger than a state.

Donor-Advised Fund. A donor-advised fund (DAF) "is a charitable giving vehicle set up under the tax umbrella of a public charity, which acts as sponsor to many funds. A donor-advised fund offers the opportunity to create a flexible vehicle for charitable giving as an alternative to direct giving or creating a private foundation. Donors receive administrative support, a cost savings and tax advantages by conducting their grantmaking through a donor-advised fund." Once the primary domain of community foundations, DAFs are now offered at major financial institutions such as Fidelity Investments, which has the largest DAF program in the country. DAFs are the fastest growing charitable vehicle. Unfortunately for grantseekers, nonprofits typically cannot apply for these funds, as the grants are recommended by the advisers to the funds.

Women's Funds. As stated in the Women's Funding Network (www .womensfundingnetwork.org):

> In the 1970s and early 1980s, following the creation of the Ms. Foundation, the idea of "women's funds"—organizations focused on

*granting money to women and girls—gained momentum. New funds
were created from regional funds like the New York Women's Foundation
to family foundations such as the Sister Fund and the Daphne
Foundation. By 2000, Women's Funding Network numbered 94 funds
with $200 million in collective assets. In the past decade, women's funds
formalized their shared values, including a commitment to a democratic
vision of philanthropy, and distilled a "social change" philosophy that
prioritizes investments capable of making lasting and proven changes in
the lives of women and girls, by fixing systems not symptoms.*

Women's funds are located in communities nationwide, and each has
its own grant guidelines.

Resource B: How to Research Funders

MOST OF THE RESOURCES an organization needs to conduct effective prospect research for funding institutions that best match the organization's programs can be found online.

The Foundation Center (http://foundationcenter.org) is rich with information and probably should be the place to begin, as it remains one of the primary sources of information on the field of philanthropy. The Center's online description of its role in philanthropy is as follows:

> *Established in 1956 and today supported by close to 550 foundations, the Foundation Center is the leading source of information about philanthropy worldwide. Through data, analysis, and training, it connects people who want to change the world to the resources they need to succeed. The Center maintains the most comprehensive database on U.S. and, increasingly, global grantmakers and their grants—a robust, accessible knowledge bank for the sector. It also operates research, education, and training programs designed to advance knowledge of philanthropy at every level. Thousands of people visit the Center's web site each day and are served in its five regional library/learning centers and its network of 450 funding information centers located in public libraries, community foundations, and educational institutions nationwide and beyond.*

The Foundation Center does provide some of the more basic foundation information for free, including each private foundation's IRS Form 990-PF. (This form, which assesses compliance with the Internal Revenue Code, lists the organization's assets, receipts, expenditures, and compensation of directors and officers, and it lists grants awarded during the previous year.)

It should be noted that this information is merely baseline data that will provide the following: contact information, type of foundation, IRS exemption status, financial data, and employer identification number (EIN).

Accessing the more comprehensive data such as previous grants, annual report information, and board and staff leadership is available for a fee through a Foundation Center resource, the Foundation Directory Online (http://fconline.fdncenter.org). According to the website of the Foundation Directory Online, it offers "the most comprehensive, in-depth information available on U.S. grantmakers and their grants, drawn from reliable sources, including IRS 990s, grantmaker websites and annual reports, plus data provided directly by grantmakers—ensuring the most accurate, timely information possible."

That said, a better option might be to go directly to the source, which is each foundation's individual website. Many foundations of all shapes and endowment sizes, as well as those foundations with no endowment, have websites containing extensive information about its leadership, theory of change, funding areas, previous grantees, and—in most instances—its grant guidelines.

There are also several respected philanthropic centers based on university campuses that provide a plethora of information, including prospect research tools and tips. Three such universities are

- The Nonprofit and Philanthropy Good Practice at the Johnson Center at Grand Valley State University. http://www.npgoodpractice.org/

- The Center on Philanthropy at Indiana University. http://www.philanthropy.iupui.edu/

- Center on Philanthropy and Public Policy at the University of Southern California. http://www.usc.edu/schools/price/research/centers/cppp.html

If Internet access is an issue, grantseekers should locate the closest Cooperating Collection. Cooperating Collections are free funding information centers in libraries, community foundations, and other nonprofit resource centers that provide a core collection of Foundation Center publications and a variety of supplementary materials and services in areas useful to grantseekers.

Should it turn out that access to a Cooperating Collection is also a challenge, go to the local library. Most public libraries will have Internet access, as well as some level of access to the Foundation Center.

Prospect research, when done correctly, should lead to the following:

- The identification of prospect foundations and corporations—those whose interests most closely match what the organization is seeking

- A comprehensive understanding of the specific interests of each prospect to better target each proposal accordingly

- The identification of any connections between the organization and one or more prospect foundations or corporations; the connection might be through someone who is on the organization's board of directors or staff or who is a volunteer or donor

Here are some steps to online funder research:

1. Identify the search criteria to be used in advance of starting the research. These can include key words, subject matter, geographic area, target audience, gender, race and ethnicity, and any other criteria that fit the organization's interests. Doing this in advance will help grantseekers in refining and targeting the research.

2. Determine the subject areas and type of support indexes (new program, capital, general operating, and so on). Those foundations and corporations that fund within the type of support being sought and that also express an interest in one or more of the subject areas are likely to be the strongest prospects. Keep an eye out for funders located in the organization's geographic area, as they are the ones most likely to give close consideration to the grantseeker's proposal.

3. Study the information on each prospect identified to learn everything possible about it, as this will allow the grantseeker to further determine whether there is truly a match.

4. Once funding sources that best match the organization's funding needs are identified, visit the foundation websites and get to know them even more. Review their annual reports, success stories of previous grants made, staff biographies, and everything else they are sharing with the public. Visiting each prospect funder's website to check guidelines is also a critical step because guidelines do change over time—and sometimes the changes are significant—but the changes may not have made their way yet into the online directory.

5. With all the information obtained from prospect funder websites, get a much clearer sense of how to target the proposals to "speak" to each funder in a language to which its program officer is likely to relate. Grantseekers will also have a grasp on how much they can reasonably request from each funder.

6. It is strongly advised that grantseekers create a prospect grid that lists every prospect identified; the organization's program that most closely aligns with each prospect's funding interests as outlined in its grant guidelines; the proposed request amount; deadline dates; and all other pertinent information. Pass this prospect list around to the

organization's board and staff to determine whether anyone has a personal contact on the board or staff of any of these prospect funders.

Here are a few additional, more creative, ways to identify funder prospects:

1. Visit the websites of nonprofit organizations that are similar in their mission, geographic area, or target audience and take a look at their donor pages. What foundations support these other organizations? Once those foundations are identified, use an Internet search engine to find out more about these potential funders.

2. Grantees should survey their surroundings. Are there any corporate headquarters close by? Or maybe franchise outlets of popular chains (of restaurants, retail stores, conveniences stores, and the like)? Contact their corporate headquarters, and find out about their corporate contribution programs—for both funding grants and in-kind support.

3. Look on the donor walls of the local hospitals, universities, and museums. Make note of the foundations and corporations that support these institutions, and then look them up online to find out more. Who knows? Grantseekers just might find a match, especially if the organization is of the same type.

4. Go to the Forum of Regional Associations of Grantmakers (www.givingforum.org) to locate the local regional association of grantmakers, and then visit that local association's website to see what resources and leads it might provide.

5. See whether a meeting can be set up with the donor relations staff person at the local community foundation. The goal is to find out more about the donor-advised funds at the community foundation and see if there are funds where the donor advisors' interests potentially match the grantseeker's programs.

Resource C: Resources for Grantseekers

Forum of Regional Associations of Grantmakers. www.givingforum.org

Foundation Search America. www.foundationsearch.com

Funders Online. www.fundersonline.org

Fundsnet Services Online. www.fundsnetservices.com

Give Spot. http://www.givespot.com/resources/grantseekers.htm

Giving to Northwestern University: Resources for Grantseekers. http://giving
.northwestern.edu/resources/grantseekers

The Grantsmanship Center. www.tgci.com

International Human Rights Funders Group: Resources for Grantseekers.
http://www.ihrfg.org/resources/grantseekers

JRS Biodiversity Foundation: Resources for Grantseekers. http://www.jrsbdf
.org/v3/GrantMakingResources.asp

Non Profit Philanthropy and Good Practice. http://www.npgoodpractice.org/

Philanthropic Ventures Foundation: Resources for Grantseekers. http://www
.venturesfoundation.org/grant-seekers/resources-for-grantseekers

Rockefeller Foundation: Links to Resources for Grantseekers. http://www
.rockefellerfoundation.org/grants/resources-grantseekers

San Diego Grantmakers: Grantseeker Resources. http://www.sdgrantmakers
.org/GrantseekerResources.aspx

Resources for Individual Grantseekers

The Bill & Melinda Gates Foundation: Grantseeking Resources for Individuals.
http://www.gatesfoundation.org/grantseeker/Pages/individuals-seeking
-grants.aspx

Foundation Center: Links for Individual Grantseekers. http://foundationcenter
.org/getstarted/individuals/

Grant Space: Resources for Individual Grantseekers. http://grantspace.org
/Tools/Knowledge-Base/Individual-Grantseekers

Prospect Resource Tools

DonorSearch. http://donorsearch.net/

The Foundation Center: Find Funders. http://foundationcenter.org
/findfunders/

GuideStar. www.guidestar.org

Logic Models

About.com: What Is a Logic Model? http://nonprofit.about.com/od
/foundationfundinggrants/f/logicmodel.htm

Center for Civic Partnerships: Logic Models/Top Tips. http://www
.civicpartnerships.org/docs/tools_resources/Logic%20Models%209.07.htm

Child Welfare Information Gateway: Evaluation Toolkit & Logic Model.
http://www.childwelfare.gov/preventing/evaluating/toolkit.cfm

Innovation Network: Point K—Tell Me More. http://www.innonet.org
/?section_id=64&content_id=185

Nonprofit Webinars: A Guide to Logic Models. http://nonprofitwebinars.com
/past_webinars/10122011-a-guide-to-logic-models-grant-writing/

Theory of Change. www.theoryofchange.org

Online Application Examples

The California Community Foundation. https://www.calfund.org/page
.aspx?pid=860

The Cleveland Foundation. http://www.clevelandfoundation.org
/GrantMaking/ApplyForAGrant/default.html

Eugene and Agnes Meyer Foundation. www.meyerfoundation.org/apply
-for-funding

The Skoll Foundation. www.skollfoundation.org

W. K. Kellogg Foundation. www.wkkf.org

Measuring Social Change, Social Justice

The Center for Effective Philanthropy: Assessment and Social Justice Funding.
http://www.effectivephilanthropy.org/blog/2010/05/assessment-and
-social-justice-funding/

Innovation Network: Measuring Social Change, Lessons from the Field.
http://www.innonet.org/index.php?section_id=6&content_id=592

Social Edge: A Program of the Skoll Foundation. http://www.socialedge
.org/discussions/success-metrics/measuring-social-impact/

Program Evaluation

Delaware Association of Nonprofits. http://www.delawarenonprofit.org
/infocentral/programeval.php

Florida Atlantic University: Nonprofit Resource Center. http://wise.fau
.edu/~rcnyhan/images/program.html

Free Management Library: Basic Guide to Program Evaluation (Including
Outcomes Evaluation). http://managementhelp.org/evaluation
/program-evaluation-guide.htm

GrantSpace: Knowledge Base. http://grantspace.org/Tools/Knowledge-Base
/Grantmakers/Program-evaluation

The James Irvine Foundation: Evaluation. http://irvine.org/evaluation
/tools-and-resources

Budget Information

The Charles Stewart Mott Foundation. http://www.mott.org
/grantsandguidelines/ForGrantees/accounting/indirectvsdirect

Nonprofit Accounting Basics: Reporting and Operations. http://www
.nonprofitaccountingbasics.org/reporting-operations/budgeting-terms
-concepts

Small Business Chron: How to Calculate Overhead for a Nonprofit.
http://smallbusiness.chron.com/calculate-overhead-nonprofit-13808.html

Government Grant Opportunities

Catalog of Federal Domestic Assistance. http://12.46.245.173/cfda/cfda.html

Grants.gov. www.grants.gov

National Endowment for the Arts. www.arts.endow.gov

USA.gov for Nonprofits. http://www.usa.gov/Business/Nonprofit.shtml

U.S. Department of Education (ED). www.ed.gov/fund/landing.jhtml

U.S. Department of Housing and Urban Development (HUD). www.hud.gov
/grants/index.cfm

Board Resources

Board Match Plus. www.boardmatchplus.org

BoardSource. www.boardsource.org

Research and Data Resources

Center on Budget and Policy Priorities. http://www.cbpp.org/

Economic Policy Institute. www.epi.org

National Center for Charitable Statistics. http://nccs.urban.org

The Opportunity Agenda. http://opportunityagenda.org/

The Urban Institute. www.urban.org

Other Resources

Alliance for Nonprofit Management. www.allianceonline.org

American Association of Grant Professionals. http://go-aagp.org

Association of Fundraising Professionals. www.afpnet.org

CharityChannel.com. www.CharityChannel.com

Chronicle of Philanthropy. www.philanthropy.com

CompassPoint. www.compasspoint.org

Council on Foundations. www.cof.org

Idealist. www.idealist.org

Philanthropy News Network.www.pnnonline.org

Women's Funding Network. www.wfnet.org

Index